The Powers of Attention, Attraction, and Intention In Field Control Therapy

My Pathway of Adventure, Discovery, and Healing:

A Practitioner's Perspective

By Steven R Tonsager, MS., LAc. And FCT Practitioner

Please see page 127 for the author's medical disclaimer.

ISBN: 978-1-946195-91-3

FUZIONPRESS
1250 E 115th Street
Burnsville, MN 55337

Dedication

I dedicate this book to my wife, Ardith. She is my sweet Valentine and my best friend and has always believed in me. This work would not have been possible without her love and inspiration, so in many ways it is really her book, too—I mean the thoughtful parts, darling, not my strange sense of humor!

Acknowledgements

How does one even start to create a list of acknowledgements? I want to say only a few things, knowing that these words will not reflect the full scope of my gratitude or come close to sharing enough names. You know who you are!

First, I want to express my thanks to the founder of Field Control Therapy, Dr. Savely Yurkovsky, because his work encouraged me to follow a path of discovery that shows no end in sight. I wish him well in his continuing work to bring FCT to its fullest potential.

I am also indebted to the brilliant minds of many others who have helped to shape my understanding of the work I do every day in the clinic. I have included their names in the book so that you may investigate their ideas for yourself! The two most important influences in my clinical work can be traced to Dr. David Hawkins and Dr. William Tiller. Again, I encourage you to learn about them for yourself.

It is also important for me to recognize and honor, as I have intended to do through my testing, all of the patients who come to me for help. There could be no discovery process without them. I am glad for the good things that have happened for so many of them and the opportunity I have for new discoveries when it is challenging to be as helpful as I would like to be.

I also want to thank Simon Rees and Kevin Eakins for the work they have done to encourage others to think differently about their health through the lens of Field Control Therapy, and I want to express my specific thanks to Simon for writing the appendix for non-FCT users. At my request, he kindly shared this with me for the benefit of those who know nothing about this therapy. Simon's writing should not be copied or distributed in any way without his permission.

I also want to thank those who agreed to read my book, especially Heidi Helgeson, and offer their feedback.

There is a way of speaking about people who come into your life that are not conventionally defined as family—as your blood relatives. Bill Tiller refers to these people as "soul family." I want to acknowledge the support that comes from my soul family and say that I hope that this book honors this family, too. I especially want to mention some of them: Fred Wagner and Sally Wright, Joe Burchik, Dave and Tina Adamek, Don Anderson and Arlene Martin, Doris Bernfeld, and Bill and Jean Tiller. Thank you.

Finally, I want to thank my wife, Ardith, for more reasons than I could ever recite. Let it simply be said that there is no greater gift to be given than to be encouraged and supported in my professional and personal life. I could not have done this without her.

Table of Contents

About the Author

Steven R Tonsager received his bachelor's degree in Chemistry from Augsburg College, Minneapolis, Minnesota in 1977 and his master's degree in Biochemistry from Michigan State University in 1979. He received his master's degree in Acupuncture and Oriental Medicine from the American Academy of Acupuncture and Oriental Medicine and then established an acupuncture clinic in River Falls, Wisconsin in 2003. Since that time, he has continued his education in Chinese medicine, cold laser therapy, homeopathy, and Field Control Therapy (FCT). He uses FCT as his primary method of helping his patients. His successful treatments produced one of the busiest FCT practices in the world and created new interest in FCT. Steve has given lectures about FCT and mentored some of its students to help with the expansion of FCT. He has written this book to be a source of practical help and encouragement to others.

My FCT Adventure: New Perspectives about Context and Application

Dear Reader,

It's time to write. Yes, I have a sense that this is the right time, and this sense comes from within. It is not because my work has been completed or because I have just made a great discovery, nor have I produced the perfect treatment results or created the newest, latest, and greatest theory. I consider myself to be wise enough to know how little I know. I also know that I am not the one who actually does any healing, but apparently I get to help out. Many appreciative patients and FCT students have encouraged me to teach and to write about my experiences and insights with FCT, so it is time because I think I know what I am capable of sharing with others and can imagine how it might be helpful. It is with this intention that I write this book.

Steve Tonsager

2/16/2014

Preliminary Comments and Intentions

Dear Reader,

I intend to write in a manner that encourages you to follow your own path, which may have little to do with my path. I hope the reading of this book will actually encourage you to do this very thing—that is, to be engaged in the adventure that I enjoy every day when I am involved in the discovery process called FCT. FCT has acquired its own meanings for me, which will become obvious to you! You will see that my words will emphasize that FCT is an adventure—not only a means of helping others, but a door to self-discovery. New perspectives emerge that are not only healing to a patient, but to us, as well. New ideas about what actually is occurring in the testing and treatment processes are invited and come to the surface for investigation and reflection. This adventure has led me to new insights and applications that have benefitted many patients.

Let me be clear that I do not intend this book to mark the launching of a new movement or school. I do not intend to discredit or criticize the work of any other FCT practitioner, especially its founder, Dr. Savely Yurkovsky. I leave it to all of you who bother to read this book to decide whether the content is of value to you or not. I am not interested in making detailed comparisons between where my FCT adventures are leading me and where others have found their best ways to utilize its theories, methodologies, and treatments. When statements are made in this book that may appear to contradict the rules and theories of others, including Dr. Yurkovsky, so be it. I will leave it to others to say, "That is not what FCT means or teaches." Opportunities for the reader to make such statements will be evident throughout the book. If it only allows you another means of identifying or clarifying your present use of FCT tools and thinking, that will be sufficient! I'm not looking for converts or followers, just that we are clear with one another.

Having said this, you may read things that probably would not pass the FCT Heresy Test. I also want to say at the outset that I am extremely grateful and appreciative of Dr. Yurkovsky's work. My thinking has been greatly influenced by his book, e-letters, e-mails, conversations, and seminars. I am pleased and honored to use his test filters and potentizer, and I believe these tools are of excellent quality. Incidentally, I encourage prospective patients who are interested in learning about FCT to go to his web site. I am hoping that these comments make it clear to you that I have great admiration and respect for his work. Without him, there would be no such animal as FCT.

Now it is time for me to inform the reader that having been armed with his tools and the tools of many others, my adventures have taken me into new territories. You, the reader, may decide if you want to follow.

Anyone who seeks greater understanding does so through the help of others and by following a personal path. We don't think, feel, or act in a vacuum. I am aware that what is written here about my discoveries and expanding perspective is strongly influenced by my own context, which includes what I have tried to learn from countless others. I have read, studied, and attended more than my fair share of books, journals, and seminars. I have been enriched by conversation from many different sources and perspectives, and I know that I have received and continue to receive plenty of boosts from the inspiration of others. I stand on the shoulders of others who have come before me. I intend to write openly about my FCT adventures, in my own occasionally irreverent manner, acknowledging whenever I remember to do so those shoulders that have given me these boosts. I hope that by my doing so, you will not think there is much in the book that is actually original. There is no intent on my part to copy the work of others without giving credit. Rather, this is my way of saying that my journey, which has been filled with new discoveries, is more about my own path and its peculiarity, as well as the necessity of timing. I think some people like to call that synchronicity. As the path has unfolded and new ideas and applications have emerged, it is probably very likely that someone, somewhere, somehow has given me another boost. Thank you.

Foreword

A human being is a system of many parts integrated into at least three main subsystems, of which two are presently invisible to our physical senses and our present-day electromagnetic measurement instruments.

My working hypothesis is that each of us is first and foremost a **soul**, indestructible and eternal, that is constructed from three domains of subtle substances that are all **superluminal** (v>c) in nature and thus invisible to present-day electromagnetic (EM) instruments. This **soul-self** requires a **biobodysuit**, or interfacing system, to experience the coarse, electrical material systems of our distance-time world of physical reality that all function at **subluminal** (v<c) U(1) Gauge state levels of nature.

The two layers of this interfacing system are (1) the inner layer, a superluminal acupuncture meridian chakra subsystem in which homeopathy and the human unconscious mind function as a template system, and (2) the outer layer, a subluminal, coarse, electric atom/molecule subsystem in which its bones, cells, neurons, and organs function.

As a simple example for illustrative purposes, let us consider the nucleation of a child's biobodysuit at the site of an egg/sperm complex in a mother's uterus:

(a) The superluminal soul encases itself in the superluminal acupuncture meridian, etc. subsystem at the egg/sperm site in the uterus,

(b) The chi (or magnetoelectric [ME]) energy flows through the meridian subsystem and **induces** electric fields and currents to flow in the egg/sperm uterus electric subluminal material subsystem,

(c) These electric currents activate the subluminal motion of electrolytes and neutral atoms/molecules in the uterus fluids, which, in turn, eventually lead to the formation of cells, neurons, etc., and

(d) Guide the development of the electric atom/molecule embryo in the uterus to eventually produce the fully formed child biobody-suit, ready to be birthed into the distance-time world of experience.

Such a child eventually needs the future services of an FCT practitioner.

To fully appreciate the unique services of a qualified FCT practitioner as compared to a qualified orthodox medical practitioner, it is now necessary to enter a discussion of the relevant thermodynamics involved in the two cases.

Most simplistically, the thermodynamic free energy difference (ΔG_{AB}) between chemical A and chemical B to form the compound A_nB_m (where *n* and *m* are integers) is directly related to the thermodynamic driving force for the chemical reaction between them (depends on exponential [$-\Delta G_{AB}/kT$], where T = absolute temperature and *k* is Boltzmann's constant in our normal U[1] Gauge symmetry state [our normal reality]).

Again, most simplistically, the U(1) Gauge state thermodynamic free energy (G), in the absence of any field effects, is given by

$$G = PV + E - TS \qquad (1a)$$

where P = pressure, V = volume, E = internal energy, T = absolute temperature, and S = entropy. The PV term was used in the old days to drive steam engines and compressors; the E term has many, many forms, two of which are nuclear reactors and atomic bombs. For constant S, the ΔT between the Earth surface and deep in the earth produces geothermal energy production. For constant T, S increases with normal human activities.

On a per mole basis, G in equation 1a becomes , and on a per atom basis, divided by Avogadro's number, N_A, yields the chemical potential μ_j for the j-species, as in

$$\mu_j = \bar{G}/N_A = \mu_0 + kT\ell n(a_j) = \mu_0 + kT\ell n(\gamma_j c_j) \qquad (1b)$$

where μ_{0j} is the standard state chemical potential for electrically neutral j-species, a_j is called the chemical activity of the j-species, ℓn is the logarithm function, c_j is the chemical concentration of j, and γ_j is called the activity coefficient of j. The c_j term produces a very local force (several atom-distances in length), while γ_j contributes a distributed force throughout the entire volume of the system.

Expanding this picture to include electrically charged species and simple field effects due to electric $\underline{E}$, magnetic $\underline{H}$, gravitational g, and stress σ fields, $\bar{G}$ changes to a generalized distance-time-only potential, ψ , given by

$$\psi = \mu_0 + kT\ell n(\hat{\gamma}_j c_j) \qquad (2a)$$

where

$$\hat{\gamma}_j = \gamma_j exp[+f(\phi, E, \underline{H}, g, \sigma)] \qquad (2b)$$

In equation (2b), the modified activity coefficient $\hat{\gamma}_j$ depends on both γ_j and the function f(……), which can be explicitly
written out (but may perhaps be more than the reader wants).

Neglecting EM Gauge symmetry state changes upon ψ in equations 2 for simplicity, we must still consider both all the **subluminal** field effects of the distance-time domain world and the **superluminal** field effects of the high dimensional domains of reality! To do this, we must expand ψ to at least conceptually include the thermodynamics of these higher dimensional domains of reality. We do this by conceptually defining a super generalized potential function, ψ^*, as

$$\psi^* = \sum_{\beta} \psi_{\beta} \ . \qquad (3)$$

Here, $\beta = 1$ is for equations (2), while $\beta = 2, 3, 4\ldots$ relate to the superluminal, higher dimensional domains of reality that include an abundance of subtle energy fields.

Orthodox medicine, in principle, has the experimental tools to explore equations (1a) and (1b), while FCT practitioners can expand the human health search to claim the territory of equations (2) and (3) investigations.

William A Tiller, Ph.D.
Professor Emeritus, Stanford University, Department of Materials Science and Engineering
(November 15, 2014)

Introduction

Some Background (But Don't Look for the Resume)

I make no promise to write in any style but my own, including my own twisted sense of humor. Let the reader beware! Now for a little background...

I find it helpful to know something about the path an author has traveled to reach the point in which it is time to write about it, so now it's time for me to give you, dear reader, a short version of what contributed to the present writing. My path, my background led me to FCT, although if you had asked me about it ten years ago, I would not have been able to even tell you what it was. I believe, nonetheless, that I am doing exactly what I need to be doing. I like where I am. Yes, I actually do. I encourage all of you to think about your basic ideas of suitability (fit), abilities, and motivation concerning FCT, because the qualities of an FCT practitioner are easily entangled with the patient.

I told you that there would be no rehearsing of a resume to convince you of my expertise to write this book, but I will say that there are at least seven influences in my personal and professional life that inform my perspectives and FCT adventures.

I am a self-starter and an avid reader who is easily motivated to explore for the purpose of seeing things more clearly and getting the big picture. I am grateful to God for a bright, inquisitive mind and sensitivity about others. I am certain that these characteristics and many others will be evident in the book.

I have some ability and experience in the hard sciences (does that make me better?) of biochemistry and toxicology, which may become evident in the book.

I have some insight to and experience in religious institutions and spiritual pathways as someone who has worked as a Lutheran minister and chaplain. I am no longer a churchgoer, but I would say that I have never been more connected to God in my entire life. It is another area in which so many shoulders have been there for me to stand upon. As you will read, for me it is inseparable from my FCT adventures.

I have some disillusionment and experience in the organization and delivery of health care because I worked as a nursing home administrator for several years. The inadequacies of our present health care model on several levels will probably be made evident in some of the words that follow. These experiences also led me to move in new directions, and I am thankful for what each aspect of my professional life is teaching me, including this one.

I have some knowledge, ability, and experience in traditional Chinese medicine from my time as an acupuncturist. I do not use needles very often anymore, but my perspectives and models about health are strongly connected to my education and experience in this world.

I also have some knowledge and experience as an FCT practitioner. I stopped counting the number of tests I've performed a few years ago, when I had conducted over 10,000 tests. Many people have been helped. Grateful patients tell others, and the snowball grows. We have not advertised for new patients in years. That statement might sound boastful to the reader, but I only intend to tell you that I have tested a lot of people—some who have benefitted by strict adherence to FCT algorithms, and others who have been benefitted by new methods and perspectives. I am happy and blessed to have been able to help them, and as I will say several times in this book, it is only God that does the healing. I am glad to be a part of it.

I have my own limited knowledge and personal experiences as a son, brother, father, husband, and friend. Perhaps you will also read between the lines and see where the FCT adventure is affected by these relationships in our personal lives as we do the work that we get to do!

These seven areas are a big part of who I am and what I bring with me to the clinic every day. You don't really ever leave them at the door of your home. I don't think you really can, or that you should. The FCT adventure can invite you into an experience of thoughtful reflection about your present interests in FCT, the source of the inner capacity to sustain this interest, and your actual and potential ability to use FCT to be helpful. This does not happen apart from who we are and where we have been.

Why am I writing this book for you? Let me remind you: If every person who came to see me was "cured," perhaps I wouldn't have been so driven to look for new answers, insights, and applications. I wouldn't work so hard to try to become a better tester or more informed about other factors influencing health. I am not easily satisfied, and I wonder if more help couldn't be provided. If only I understood a little more, investigated a little more, tried harder, worked harder…You get the picture! Given my nature, as alluded to in the comments about my background, what has been taking place in my psyche and in the clinic is not very surprising. I just want things to get better. I just want FCT to be even more helpful. The motivations behind this book should be clear to you: To be more helpful to my patients, to experiment with modifications to the testing procedures and methods of creating remedies, to consider other perspectives to deepen understanding, to simplify or alter processes that might help others to learn how to improve their FCT skills, and to develop new applications. I intend my book to contribute and connect to all of these motivations!

CHAPTER ONE

Being More Helpful to Patients

Let's start with being more helpful to patients. Besides being more competent and successful in terms of patient outcomes (to state the obvious), I find there are several things that are helpful: What we say, how we say it, and making the process of FCT testing (which is strange to most people) more real to the patient are important.

What We Say

FCT is a foreign language, reminiscent of the same description my organic chemistry teacher gave me forty years ago when I began to learn the nomenclature as a college student. You need to find a language—in the form of pictures and analogies—that can help patients develop an idea of what you are doing and why you are doing it. I have several of these analogies that I have shared with patients, and I have offered several of them to FCT practitioners to try on for size. A couple of examples:

Patient: What is in that vial? I don't understand how it can work.

Yours truly: There is information in the vial in a form that your body's intelligence can understand. If your body is the result of the carrying out of specific instructions from its informational fields, we can help your body via providing useful information. Sometimes the information the body needs to be healthy has been affected by a disease or exposure to a chemical, kind of like when your computer gets attacked by a virus. If you find a computer virus, you need to run software to eliminate the virus and reinstall the software. FCT is something like that. If we fix any problems that are in the instructions for how the body needs to work, it can work better.

Yours truly: On a lighter note, when my daughter Alyssa was asked by a friend of hers what she was taking, she responded by saying that she didn't know exactly what it was. "My daddy gives me these vials. I take drops under my tongue. I get better. They're like little messages in water." No one can fully explain how it works, so Alyssa's explanation is just perfect. We are remarkably created, and water that has been imprinted with the right information can be used by our bodies (which are mostly a type of water) for communication, by which the whole body can be helped. If you're really interested in this subject, there are plenty of intriguing books about the properties of water. Check out the pictures of Dr. Masuru Emoto or the writings of Dr. Mae-Won Ho. That would be a place to start dreaming about water.

Yours truly: On another note, think of your CD player. How does it work? Think of your body as a CD player. The vial that I'm going to give you is kind of like a CD. When you take your drops, you are loading a series of CDs that your body will play. Does your CD player work well if it's dirty? Of course not! What do you do? Clean it. What interferes with your body's ability to play CDs? Lots of stuff, including electromagnetic interference from technology and other sources that make it difficult for your body to play the CDs. When interference from cellphones, computers, iPads, or other devices is affecting you, it's kind of like your CD player getting dirty and in need of a cleaning. If you do not avoid these technologies, when you're taking your drops, you might have sufficient interference that you will have an EMF block. In other words, the treatment might not work. There are other things you can do to prevent your body from having its informational fields and the rest of you "scrambled," so let me tell you about MEMON transformers, which can help keep your CD player clean.Patient: I don't get what you're doing when you hold my ankles. What do you feel? What does that have to do with my health?

Yours truly: Those are good questions. This is very different than what you're used to, but information about your health is accessible through this testing. This test can tell us things about your health that is not evident in blood, urine, stool, or saliva tests. We have a different window through which to see things in a different way. Your body tells on you! We have many different filters to look at different aspects of your health and what is affecting it through a non-physical means called bio-resonance. If you're interested in learning more about it, I can give you some places to look. When we're done with the testing, we will goof off a little bit and I will show you how responsive you are to what I'm discovering about you through the testing. I think you'll find it interesting and fun. Most people who come here are a little disappointed if I don't say or show them something that is a little strange, so let me finish testing you and then I will show you what I mean. (The testing is often a simple AK test which supports an FCT finding.)

More about What We Say

I am more helpful and probably more credible to patients because of a background in biochemistry, toxicology, and Chinese Medicine and my continued study of developments in orthodox biochemically based medicine. It is important, but it is not the whole story. I will discuss this topic later, when I discuss new applications. The reason that I bring it up now is that it is very helpful to the patient (and sometimes to your own testing process) to understand the diagnoses and etiologies that bring them knocking at your door.

Be respectful of the advice and treatment that has already been received by the patient, but consider placing it in a new context. Be certain that you have also covered your own backside with signed documentation stating that you are not taking on the supervision of medications, other medical treatments, giving them a conventional diagnosis, or directing them to ignore medical advice from medical specialists. This statement also obviously applies to this book, by the way. It is not intended to be a medical book or a substitute for medical advice and treatment.

Let me try to give an example of some of the things I might consider saying.

Patient: My doctor says that I have arthritis...I'm getting old. He gave me some medication I can take for pain and swelling, and it helps my symptoms.

Yours truly: Your doctor tells you that you have arthritis. I'm curious. Did he say what kind of arthritis you have? We're all getting older, but maybe there are some causes for the arthritis besides getting older. Maybe we could treat these causes so that you would not need the medication. I'm not telling you to stop taking your medicine, but medicines frequently have side effects, so if we could find out what is causing the pain in your joints, maybe you would feel better.

Patient: That would be wonderful.

Yours truly: So, let's test you and focus on your joints and any organs that might have a special influence on your joints. Let's look at your joints through the FCT testing for any signs of infection, toxicity, or nutritional deficiency. You might say that we have a different kind of lens in FCT, so we are able to look for other things. I will tell you what the findings are and then we can see if they might relate to your joints or any other health problems we've not talked about.

The conversations vary in content, but hopefully not in intent, which is to meet the patient where he or she chooses to be met, whether it be a cold or cancer or depression. Do not make promises that you cannot keep. Be clear about what you are seeking to discover and to help. Do not denigrate the efforts made by others on behalf of the patient. Do not criticize the choices the patient has already made to try to become well. You have a different lens from which to view health, and it may be helpful. When you test the patient, you are entering a sacred place. Give the credit for any improvements to God.

One More Thing about What We Say

Let's not add to the burden of being blamed for an illness or a decline in health that many patients often carry. Illness is an opportunity for great things to happen according to a timing about which I admit to being mostly clueless. It has its own logic and momentum. According to my testing, it is certainly true that we are subject to what we hold in mind. (I told you that there would be mention of many strong shoulders upon which I stand—thank you, Dr. David Hawkins.) There is a time and place for self-examination when it comes to any kind of suffering and its meaning. Meeting people where they are at, not where you think they should be, is kind and compassionate.

Compassion comes from within us when we stop judging and evaluating others, when we know that we are not standing in someone else's shoes and are incapable of doing so! We are mostly small minded and clueless, but it is all that we know. Each patient comes with a level of consciousness, a box of a particular size beyond which things are not understood or considered. The unity behind all expressions of the Source of our existence, in its infinite variety (including the patients, of course), is made visible when our spiritual vision is restored through love, peace, and joy. Let it emanate from you when you speak with your patients. (More about other consequences of this intention to follow.)

Making What We Say a Bit More Real

Much has been written about applied kinesiology, and I am not an expert. I learned applied kinesiology through my own study of its well-known authors. I also became a certified Brimhall practitioner, a training course taken mostly by chiropractors that uses adjustors, cold lasers, some other toys, and applied kinesiology. Learning to use my hands to scan acupuncture meridians for troubles helped me to improve my skills, too. I bring it up here because these techniques have been beneficial to patients for several important reasons. Again, following are a few examples to illustrate what I mean. If you'd like, dear reader, you can come up with your own versions that might help others to be open to new ways of thinking about what you do and why you are doing it!

First Example of Making it Real

Yours truly: Did you have any breakfast today?

Patient: Yes, I ate a couple of hours ago.

Yours truly: (*My hands and attention are ready for testing.*) What did you have this morning?

Patient: I had toast (*stress*), an egg (*stress*), and black coffee (*no stress*). Why?

Yours truly: Because I think that your breakfast didn't agree with you. Your body has a hard time with wheat, and probably other gluten-containing grains, and egg whites. It's telling on you.

Patient: How do you know that?

Yours truly: Because your body is in what I would call alarm state. There is stress in your system from your breakfast that I am able to detect. This stress will be there for several hours—at least four hours, and maybe more. Let me show you what I mean.

(There are many ways to do this. I will mention only one: Localize the most stressed GI location from breakfast. The location will depend on how long ago the meal was consumed. Let's say it was two hours ago—the stress will be easily picked up in the small intestine. If you're not sure, use one of the SI vials to find it. Scan with your hand if you know how to do this, or use your knowledge of anatomy to identify a suitable location.)

Yours truly: Depending on when you ate your breakfast, we can identify where the stress is the greatest. Do you mind if I touch your abdomen?

Patient: No, I don't. Go ahead.

Yours truly: Well, let me see if you're testable. (*Again, you have many options. Here's one: Use the patient's arm, with the elbow locked so that the strong muscles of the forearm and upper arm are not engaged to isolate the shoulder. This is an easy and time-efficient way to do this when time is precious!*) Keep your arm straight. When I push on your arm, you resist. You will get weak when I do certain things. When you feel your arm weaken, stop resisting and let your arm come down so that you don't hurt your shoulder. You could be a lineman for the Green Bay Packers, but if there's something stressing you, you're going to get weak and your arm will want to come down! You're probably a lot stronger than me, but it's not a contest of strength. Your body knows what weakens it and what makes it strong. I think you will find this interesting and fun! Are you ready?

Patient: Sure.

Yours truly: Strong as you can be. Resist. (*The arm is strong and intact. Now the index finger of my other hand touches the Yin Tang point.*) Resist. (*The patient goes weak.*)

Patient: How did you do that? (*The patient smiles mostly, like "what did you just do"?*)

Yours truly: That means you're normal. Let's do it again so that you can trust the difference.

Patient: That's really cool. (*I've also heard strange, amazing, weird, and "Oh, my chiropractor did that to me."*)

Yours truly: Now let's test kidney 27—the acupuncture point, not where your kidneys are located. (*They are strong and intact.*) Good. You are testable. What we're doing is different from FCT, but it will help to reinforce some of the things that we're talking about and what the testing is telling me.

Patient: Okay.

Yours truly: This is a vial made from egg whites. I will put it here over your Ren meridian. (*We're in the vicinity of the thymus.*) Resist. (*The patient's arm weakens and goes down.*) I don't think your body handles those egg whites too well. Let's try a vial of gluten. (*Same result.*) I don't think your body likes the gluten very well, either. These foods don't agree with you. You will be healthier and feel better if you can be compatible with what you eat. Many people who are a lot smarter than me have said that food is the first medicine. Do you feel bloated sometimes? Are your bowels sluggish? Do your joints ache? (*You fill in the rest…*) Maybe changing your diet might help. You could give it a try and see if you feel better.

Patient: I probably could eat differently—it's just that this is what I've usually had for breakfast for most of my life.

Yours truly: I get it. We can try one more thing to see if we could help you to be more compatible with what you're used to eating. Maybe you would have managed your food better if it had been harmonized before eating with a MEMON Food Harmonizer. I've found that it's possible to use the MEMON Food Harmonizer after you've eaten to help your system to handle the food and the breakdown products of your food, as well. (*MEMON transformers will be discussed in a later section of the book.*) Let's see what we can do…Do you mind if I touch your abdomen?

Patient: No, I don't. Go ahead.

Yours truly: (*Now testing patient's arm with my left hand and my right hand on the most stressed area. Again, the location is dependent on how long ago the food was consumed. For purposes of illustration, let's say that the peak of the stress is intestinal and around the navel. I place my right hand on the area over his navel and apply force to the raised right arm of the patient using my left hand. He goes weak.*) There's weakness here according to my testing; it is in the small intestine. Let's see if we can do something about it. (*I place the MEMON Food Harmonizer on the stressed area.*) Sometimes this MEMON transformer placed over the stressed area will eliminate the stress. I will set a timer for four minutes and then we will check it again. The MEMON transformer is intended to be used prior to consumption, but I have often found it to be very helpful if you've eaten something that your body has a problem with. The MEMON transformer harmonizes foods and liquids. You put the food or beverage on top of the card. The card has a projection zone of about nine inches and will harmonize things stored in glass, plastic, cardboard, and ceramic containers, but not in glasses or bowls made of metal. Since you don't have a metal plate in your abdomen, I think this might help. (*I might do some additional testing or answer some other questions about the MEMON Food Harmonizer while we are allowing sufficient time for possible harmonization. Four minutes passes.*)

Yours truly: Let's see what's happened. Do your intestines (*bowels, stomach, ovaries, etc.—there are many potential outcomes*) feel better and more relaxed? (*Very often, the patient will feel the difference—more about this in another section of the book.*)

Patient: Yes, I do feel better.

Yours truly: Let's retest. (*I repeat the testing, placing my hand over the stressed area where the patient was previously weak. Alternatively, you can track the changes with the FCT testing apparatus, using the muscle testing only to help solidify what the patient is already feeling and to encourage adoption of a more compatible diet.*) You're strong.

Patient: That's amazing.

Yours truly: I'm glad you feel better. That tells me that you would probably feel better if you avoided or limited the foods that I mentioned. However, if you harmonized the food prior to consumption or harmonized the area in your GI tract where the stress was being experienced like we just did, you would feel better—that location could be determined according to your symptoms and how long ago you ate.

Patient: That's very cool.

This is one of many examples of many different types that illustrate the importance of making things more real to the patient.

Second Example of Making it Real

FCT testing indicates that your patient has a tick-borne illness affecting many different aspects of the patient's health. You could pick one pathogen (*typically there are at least a few co-infections*) on one site (*although there are typically several relevant sites*) and use an AK technique to make the testing more real and encourage the patient. I have experience with many scenarios. The patient may come to you wondering what is causing the health problems, having some suspicion that it might be "Lyme's," or having been treated for "Lyme's" by alternative medicine, conventional medicine, or both. Here is one way, among many variants, that I have used to help the patient become engaged with the testing and treatment!

Yours truly: According to my testing, your health is being affected by a tick-borne illness. I think that you are being affected by the spirochete, or *borrelia burgdorferi*, which is what people usually mean when they are talking about "Lyme's," but also by a second pathogen called *babesia*. I checked you for many other co-infections, but according to my testing, these other pathogens are not an issue.

(*Patient responses vary. Some are distressed at the idea that tick-borne illness is affecting their health, and others are relieved to have an answer or a confirmation of suspicions. Others are surprised, because multiple rounds of antibiotics alleviated many symptoms, so he or she must have been cured! This can be an opportunity, as with any illness, infection, or other pernicious agent, to think as broadly as you are capable of to help make it real. Here's one way, of the many ways that I've used to do this.*)

Yours truly: Let me show you with a different kind of test how *borrelia* and *babesia* are affecting you. (*Pick any one of the many targets that has become obvious through your testing and the patient's symptoms. Do the preliminary testing procedure mentioned in the first example to ensure that the patient is testable.)*

Yours truly: When something is affecting your health, it will cause stress, and your body will tell on you. In other words, your arm is going to go weak. This is the vial for *borrelia*. Let's see how your body responds to it. (*Place it over the thymus. The body goes weak.*) This is the vial for *babesia*. Let's check your response to it, also. (*Place it over the thymus. The body goes weak.*) According to the testing, these are the two co-infections that are affecting your health. We want to get rid of these influences—tell them to take a hike. Let's try this vial. This is a vial for bartonella. According to my testing, you don't have it. (*Place it over the thymus. The body stays strong.*) Do you feel the difference?

Patient: Yes, I don't weaken to it at all.

Yours truly: That's because *bartonella* is not a problem. If we can develop a protocol and make remedies to clear you of the influence of *borrelia* and *babesia*, we should be able to eliminate its effects on your health. When I retest you, you should be as strong to the *babesia* and *borrelia* as you are to the *bartonella*. I will check you with my FCT testing, as well, which I think is much more sensitive than this simple muscle test. We will know that this has been eliminated as an influence on your health.

Patient: That sounds great.

Yours truly: Let me show you one more thing about this. I think you will find it interesting. One of your big complaints is that your joints are sore, especially your knees. According to the testing, the *borrelia* is the main reason your knees are bothering you. Let's goof off some more.

Patient: Okay.

(The patient places his/her arm up in the testing position again. You will use your left hand to check arm strength—the intactness of the muscle, if we need to say it differently for some of you, but let's not split hairs. Put your right hand on the patient's knee. Say "knee" out loud if you want to make everything very clear about your intent. The arm will go weak.)

Yours truly: Let's see how addressing the *borrelia* can help your knees. Resist.

Patient: I can't resist. I'm weak.

(You have several options. You can put the borrelia vial in your hand and now place your hand on the patient's knee, or you could have the patient hold the vial in his hand. You're getting ready to challenge the knee again with a technique that has sometimes been called two pointing.)

Yours truly: I am placing the *borrelia* vial under my hand and over your knee. Eliminating the stress to your knees, as well as to the rest of your body, will be helped by clearing you of the influence of *borrelia;* I think that your knee will now be stronger. Resist. (*The patient is strong.*)

Patient: That's amazing. How did you do that? (*Remember, we're just trying to make it real!*)

Yours truly: Your body knows what's bothering it. I'm just trying to show you that if we can eliminate the stress caused by tick-borne illness, you should feel better in a lot of ways, including your knees.

This exercise takes longer to explain than to do. For most patients, it opens the door to an experience that is completely foreign to them, but no less foreign to them than the idea that putting a bunch of vials on a plate while holding a metal rod should serve any useful purpose. It is also certainly no less foreign than the idea that taking a few drops under the tongue every now and then should help them to feel better—a good reason for one of my patients to kindly refer to them as voodoo drops! When wonderful things happen (and I wish it was all of the time), give the credit to God and the healing capacities within all of us. Perhaps our best efforts amount to only a form of encouragement to help the patient do what was just hidden to them before. Maybe their box got a little bigger.

I have illustrated a couple of the ways that I have used AK to make it more real for my patients. (I will say more about engaging the patient's mind and intent in testing in later sections.) These two examples could be varied in many ways, but the idea is the same—helping the patient feel that everything you are saying and doing is more real. You can probably come up with better ways to do this for yourself, and I strongly encourage you to do just that.

CHAPTER TWO

Modifications of Testing Procedures

Dear readers, I may be treading on sacred ground throughout this book, including this very moment. In this section, I will be offering some alternative testing procedures that I have found to be helpful. These modifications are, as FCT theory and practice can also attest to in its development, a work in progress. This is evidenced in FCT orthodoxy as the emergence of new filters for pathogens and tissues as well as new interpretations and discoveries through new cases. I like to refer to these developments as upgrades of my mental software. Thanks to so many patients, testing opportunities, study, investigation, and meditation, there have been several upgrades! I hope there will be many more.

Let me put it to you this way: You can't find what you don't realize is missing. Consider the possibility that there are important qualities and larger contexts into which the FCT model can be expanded beyond its present scope. We have an ability to do this with the tool called intention—"our own personal mouse," as I like to refer to it. Intention combined with attention to undiscovered (but discoverable) information offers you a one-way ticket to a place or a new attraction that you may have never visited before. This is a discovery process that can never end. It offers you the opportunity to set aside any limiting beliefs about health, both how to identify and treat any negative influences and how to encourage greater health of body, mind, soul, and spirit. If this is pseudoscience, then so be it. More about this topic to follow—yes, I'm trying to encourage salivation, not salvation! Let's not forget where the tickets come from.

One example of a potentially limiting belief system (it's only potential because it depends on the belief system of a particular individual or practitioner) is that all of the necessary information about a certain organ, tissue, or pathogen is to be found in its corresponding filter. The belief continues that when a remedy is made using this particular filter, it will provide all the relevant elements concerning the meaning of the filter. This is a belief system that is reinforced in the testing process, when the filter is used to generate a response measured by the tester. It is likely that this belief is held in mind, and therefore the practitioner is subject to it. As others have often said, "We are subject to what we hold in mind." Therefore, the interpretation of a stress response or lack of a response concerning any one of the FCT moves is also an exercise that reinforces the FCT belief system.

I believe that these beliefs may prevent us from being prepared to be attentive and attracted to other things because of contextual limitations. Contrary or complementary beliefs discovered through experimentation with testing modifications should not be measured against whether they sound, smell, or taste like FCT, but on the responses of the patient. Favorable responses require, or at least encourage, expansion of beliefs. Intention gives you a one-way ticket to any destination. Yes, dear reader, it is a one-way ticket because once you get started, there's no going back.

To reiterate, the purpose of this book is not to go over the established "moves," testing algorithms, and derived protocols that arise from a typical test. This information is available from others and is in good hands through Simon Rees and Kevin Eakins, wonderful people with great integrity. I am pleased to know them, and I thank them for all their good work and dedication to FCT. What I intend for you to consider is the possibility of additional testing procedures that I am using (in addition to the orthodox methods) that have been beneficial. Here we go!

Why Bother to Even Try to Modify?

It's not an unimportant question. The answers are perfectly simple and straightforward. Here is one obvious way to express this answer: Not every patient is "cured" (or becomes as well as one might hope for). I suppose you could conclude that it was the skill of the practitioner that limited the outcome or that the patient has met the limits of what is possible in terms of recovery of health. I suppose one could also say that the theory and/or testing procedures of FCT are helpful, but not infallible or complete as far as its ability to understand the patient's troubles and offer a solution or a perfect solution.

I have been able to be of help to many people, but not to everyone. I have said goodbye to patients whom I grew to love very much and are now in God's hands, and I have shared my sorrows with their families. Perhaps the limits on what could have been done to help them were reached, or nearly so, but perhaps not. I take great comfort that, as the scriptures say, "Even the hairs on your head are numbered." Yes, our days are numbered. At least, that is what I think. My work is about trying to add or rediscover qualities in the lives of my patients that have been affected by stresses: Physical, emotional, mental, and spiritual. I am thankful for the one-way ticket to see if I can do more to help others, but I do so with the assurances that God will ensure my safety and know exactly where it is that I need to go. Think about it.

Okay, back to the nitty-gritty, although you can see where this thought process might lead me! The intent of helping my patients as much as possible led me to think about the algorithm itself and not only the usefulness, but the comprehensiveness of the degenerative and stress organ filters. The approach was proven through my testing and the outcome associated with taking the remedies to be very useful, but not in all cases. I wondered if something was being missed in the testing. What was really being measured, and what was not? I wondered if the testing was at times very accurate to the requirements imposed by the algorithm, but missed the mark in terms of what the patient was seeking or needed.

I conducted my own inquiries into the nature of these organizing filters and some of their properties. I compared these findings to others that could be generated by modifying the testing procedures. This was interesting and compelling because when I ventured outside the FCT boundaries, there were many interesting discoveries. I intend to express these discoveries in different ways with the hope that perhaps one of them will pique your interest...or salivation. Let's get strange first and move to the more concrete after that.

I discovered that every organizing filter could be represented by a number or a combination of other filters. Moreover, the numbers could be simplified with an interesting kind of math that reduces numbers to a single digit. (These numbers are not included in this book.) The numbers for the degenerative filters could be placed in the testing sequence and would represent the Schumann resonance. How strange is that? How fun is that?

The degenerative filters were developed from homeopathic methods using parasympathetic tissues. For example, it was found that when stress to the parasympathetic system is reduced by MEMON transformers to eliminate geopathic stress, patients become calmer and typically sleep better. These filters can be represented, at least in part, by a series of numbers. Apparently, these resonances impact parasympathetic aspects of the autonomic nervous system. The potencies of the parasympathetic tissue that are reflected in the degenerative filters also reflect mathematical relationships that are further reflected at many different levels—both microcosmic and macrocosmic, to be sure—and physical, energetic, and informational domains. Wow! I recognized and discovered that some of the representative numbers held significant meaning in other circles of seekers, healers, and researchers regarding particular frequencies of important biogeometries, scales, and tones. That was just a coincidence, right?

I also found that I could use filters for crystal, photon, color, and sound from the kit of FCT filters to reproduce these numbers and the fifteen filters. I found that in testing numbers, symptoms, and disease states/conditions, the associative principle in mathematics does not apply: For example, 1+4 does not equal 4+1 in this case. We are not dealing with the rules of Abelian Algebra here. Each experiment, each test, changes the terrain to be tested. If you choose to begin in a particular place, you will end in a particular place. If you begin somewhere else, you may find yourself in another state or country at the end. It really does matter where you begin; it seems more than reasonable to ask if the first match in the algorithm is always the best place from which to depart. I found that when you started in a different place, the process could take you more places than you might have guessed…So much for all of those years of thinking that a bunch of numbers always produced the same sum. Here I'm reminded of another very interesting scientist, the late Dr. Peter Fraser, and his theories about the structure of the biofield and the importance of sequence. Good shoulders! I recommend that you read his books and learn about his inventions.

These new places you end up in would encourage further reflection about the significance of the destination and whether or not it was really where you needed to go, after all. For me, this mathematical play and the speculation around any significance continues to be quite intriguing. This is a work in progress. I am a work in progress. Caution is advised. Wait for Volume Two!

With each discovery, I descended further into the rabbit hole. Emerging quite furry from each descent, I saw the testing differently than before. I thought that the ascending potencies of parasympathetic tissue in the degenerative organ filters and the ascending potencies of sympathetic tissue in the stressed organ filters were only one means of assessing the health of the patient and what kinds of remedies would be most useful. I also wondered if everyone should get on the train and punch the ticket according to these schedules. Maybe someone needed a different route and destination! These kinds of findings only encourage someone like me to keep digging, hunting, and scavenging. My intuition encouraged me to think that there might be other categories, or criteria, than the FCT guiding filters to describe the obstacles toward improved health—and not just from a physical perspective. Perhaps a new railroad or carrier could help people see some other sites with great benefit. On the other hand, those same people might let everyone know through their Trip Advisor site that this was a waste of time.

Modification Time: Selective Use of the Fifteen Filters and Upgrades

As I have more than hinted at, the more one plays and ponders, the more one wonders if something could be missing. The more one tests, the more one develops a sense of what kinds of information will be forthcoming—which is quite different from controlling the outcome. Here is one modification of the testing procedure that works very well for me: This is a simplification of the typical algorithm. Instead of placing each of the fifteen filters on the plate in the prescribed order and using the accepted moves of the FCT chess game, your focus is on whether or not to include a particular filter. Include Degenerative Organ Number 1? No. Include Degenerative Organ Number 2? No. Include Degenerative Organ Number 3? Yes. Location? Reasoning? Toxicity? Infection? Radiation?...Do you get it? There may be stress to many of the fifteen kingdoms, but the patient only needs to pay taxes to some of them. Yes, this really works. Try it.

Here is another testing modification: Run through the algorithm or a modification such as the one that I just mentioned. Ask if the treatment can be improved. Is it done? You will be surprised that long after you've visited the fifteenth Lord of the kingdoms (five degenerative organs and ten stressed organs), there can be others who want a visit. (I believe Dr. Yurkovsky still uses stealth filters to find out who has been overlooked.) If you calibrate the accuracy of your testing and the efficacy of your treatment (I will discuss this later in the book), you will find that it is possible to increase the calibration (and presumably the usefulness) of your treatment by adding this additional step.

Does this make a difference? Find out for yourself. Very good things can happen following the current testing methods (algorithms), but I believe there is the potential to uncover additional relevant information by setting aside these guidelines—swimming outside the markers that warn you of the deep water! I think there are other helpful starting points from which to test that will take you on other paths outside of the safety ropes. Remember, since the rules of Abelian Algebra do not apply, you can wind up in a very different place. The vectors are different. The tensors are different, but no more about this until the next book, and no numbers or equations, either! If you want to explore the relevance of vectors and tensors as part of a model to represent mathematically the impact of intention on D space and R space, you will not find it in this book. You will need to consult the work of Dr. Tiller. Some of his work is listed at the end of the book.

Using the methodologies described by Dr. David Hawkins, I have calibrated the overall levels of FCT practitioners, FCT as method and theory, and many of my own tests and treatments to learn that there is much to be gained by working to increase the power of FCT, which is more heresy, I have no doubt, but like I said, I'm travelling on a one-way ticket.

Other Organizing Concepts to Reconfigure Testing

Here's another testing wrinkle: I ask patients to write on the intake form their reason(s) for coming to see me. Since I'm trying to stand in the shoes of my patients, it seems understandable that my conversation, testing, and treatment should connect with their reason for coming in the first place. Duh! From this point of view, I don't believe I have donned an allopathic coat, but perhaps if I look into my closet, I might spot one buried in the back. Let me try to illustrate this to you with some examples.

My patient is in his early sixties and has been diagnosed with and is on medication for high blood pressure. He doesn't feel especially great, complaining of fatigue, chronic pain, and worry about his heart. He is quite clear that his reason for coming is his high blood pressure. Do we have to talk him out of his reason for coming?

I created several vials over the past years for symptoms and medical conditions that for reasons that will be explained later I refer to as H vials. In this case, I use my H vial for hypertension. The stress, or what I like to refer to as an incoherency reading, is 240—that's a high number for this kind of test. (I will also explain later in the book how this number is derived.) I "ask" in my testing about the contributing stresses that create a reading of 240 and find that this includes EMF, geopathic stress, toxicity, and infection. Inclusion of these factors reduces the reading to thirty. This can be done by either using the platform or not using it, but more about this heretical practice will be offered to you later.

Identifying these causative factors gives me good reason to believe that if each of them can be more specifically identified and treated (with appropriate support), hypertension should be reduced and medications might be reduced or eliminated. Remember to give no medical advice unless you're licensed and qualified to do so. I will try to express this more clearly in a later section, but for now, let's go to dialogue mode.

Yours truly: I think there are several things that are contributing to your high blood pressure. If we can treat them in the order your body asks for help, maybe we can eliminate the reasons for your high blood pressure. You might be able to cut back or eliminate the medication you're taking.

Patient: That would be great.

Yours truly: According to the testing, one of the things that is affecting your blood pressure is electromagnetic radiation. Let's see how much it is bothering you and see what happens if we try to neutralize its effects. According to the testing, your hypertension could be reduced by using MEMON transformers to reduce the stress from technology and geopathic stress. (*I then muscle test them with vials reflective of both EMF stress and geopathic stress—there are many choices to pick from. Give the patient the chance to experience the stress this causes. Two-point it, if you like, to the heart.*) I'm going to have you hold a CAR B MEMON in your hand for five minutes and put a body transformer on your wrist. We will recheck your responses and see how you feel after the time has expired. (*Five minutes goes by while you test other items of interest.*) Let's recheck you. (*Now the patient tests strong when challenged to these stresses and the heart tests stronger. You recheck the H vial, reading for hypertension, and now the balance is 120.)* Clearing you of this stress has a very positive effect on your blood pressure. I will finish my testing and let you know what my findings are. If we can identify other influences and treat them with remedies too, good things can happen.

Patient: That sounds great.

Here's an anxiety example to follow: An H vial for anxiety gives an indication of how powerful this type of influence is to the patient. You can establish a value or level first, and for purposes of illustration, it is 300. That's very high and probably signifies that anxiety is a major struggle and a dominant factor in the patient's self-understanding of what is affecting him/her. Organize your testing around anxiety using the fifteen Lords, the lords to whom taxes must be paid, or venture out on your own and ask which of them needs to be acknowledged. Every approach can work, but it is very possible that everyone who tests has access to the dealmakers and breakers, so you may have to visit everybody. Since the associative principle of mathematics does not apply, introduce the patient's problem of anxiety into the mix first. Let it be your starting point, the train station from which you depart. Once you have done this, a course can be set from where you begin. You will be told what the stops are and if work needs to be done at any or many of the stops to accommodate the passengers. Not all of them welcome. Evaluate the importance of each stop and tell the patient where you think you might be going.

For this patient, a woman in her late thirties, we will be visiting bird land and a fungus-filled town from far away. She will handle everything better if she can appreciate that her iPad and home Wi-Fi are not exactly her friends. Exposure and treatment for EMFs with MEMON devices during the testing, as described, is calming, and you have determined with before and after measurements the importance of electromagnetic smog and similar influences. You determine that this intervention reduces your 300 value to 180. She tells you that she feels considerably calmer after being treated with MEMON. If you have time, do a muscle challenge to help bring her more on board to the influence of *psittaci* and *Coccidiodes immitis* to her health and, specifically, to her anxiety. With compassion flavored with gentle humor as the situation presents itself, you tell her that it is time to "de-bird brain her" and that you expect that this way, there will be greater calm and muscles that are more responsive to her. You tell her that her body told on her: Her trip to Arizona a couple of winters ago gave her more than a tan. A windy day shared a common fungus from the region that can affect a person in many ways, including heightening anxiety.

When the situation is appropriate, reinforce your findings with additional information you know about the significance of the findings (you cannot find what you cannot imagine, much less explain something if you know nothing about it) through conversation or reinforce their importance through muscle testing. Patients do better when you have tried to share some perspective about the relevance of your findings to an overall concern they have about their health.

Another Mapping Tool

The previous examples were intended to lead into the idea that the FCT filters, as well as other filters, can be used to develop a sense of the importance of a particular problem and the relative importance of various factors regarding the problem. This can be done by focusing on the pernicious factors. Of equal importance is the fact that this can be done by focusing on the organs/tissues that are relevant to the problem. An additional step can be taken by asking which pernicious factor or organ/tissue is the most important and needs to be treated first for what reason, and so on and so forth. What limits you? Only your ability to conceive a clear question or statement and receive the answer will hold you back. Remember, it is a one-way ticket—you have a mouse to take you anywhere. Of course, there are plenty of opportunities for error.

I am encouraging you to think that FCT provides you with a tool—not the only available tool, but a valid tool to ask many questions. In my opinion, insufficient attention is given to an aspect of any FCT testing referred to by some as mental radiesthesia. (I hope that doesn't offend anyone.) I don't care what you call it, but I'm speaking of those aspects of testing that are used to establishing the timing and frequencies of remedy administration...not to mention the remote testing, which is used by many practitioners (including its inventor). This is not a criticism, but a practice about which I will be making some comments. One of the weaknesses in the teaching and discussion of FCT testing and theory is a lack of discussion about the complementing roles and perspectives of what is referred to as physical radiesthesia and mental radiesthesia. One perspective suggests that the former refers to a higher science connected to quantum mechanics and biophysics, while the other sends some people searching for references to the occult and other unwelcomed company. This is unfortunate...Yes, that was an editorial comment on my part! I get to do that. It's my book. I am not trying to represent the opinions of others or the official positions of FCT, just so we're clear. Right?

Engaging the Patient's Cooperation and Intent: Locations, Factors, Timing, and Place

Dear Reader: This is so much fun to do, and very helpful. There are several variations and ways to play this game that I think are extremely helpful. Here are a few examples that can help you be more accurate in your testing regarding stressed or diseased locations/tissues, what might be causing the stress, as well as when, and where it may have originated.

Patient Helps to Specify the Location

The patient comes in to see you because of a sore right shoulder.

Patient: My shoulder is sore. It really bothers me after I shovel the snow. It didn't bother me like this last year. I went to my doctor, and he told me that it was arthritis and that maybe it's time to get someone else to do the shoveling. He told me that I could try some Tylenol or ibuprofen—you know, over-the-counter stuff. If that didn't help, we could try a cortisone shot. It does help when I take Tylenol and don't work my shoulder too hard.

(There is a bunch of stuff you might ask, and I often do, to help you better understand the problem. Is it relieved by cold, heat, or massage? I might also palpate for tenderness and do some tests to check the rotator cuff, have him demonstrate what positions and motions aggravate the pain, and so on and so on, but the present purpose for including this illustration is for the patient to give me a different kind of help.)

Yours truly: Let's try a couple of things to see if we can better specify where the pain is strongest and if it's coming from the shoulder or someplace else. Maybe your doctor is right and you have arthritis, but maybe, if we can identify more precisely the source of the pain we can find some other causes. I'm not sure getting another year older is the only reason that the shoveling is so hard on you this year. Maybe you need to move south, away from the snow. If I had Florida in a bottle, maybe I should give that to you!

Do you feel the pain right now?

Patient: I do, but not as bad as after I've been shoveling. I also took two Tylenol last night to help me sleep.

Yours truly: So here's what I want you to do: Focus on where you're feeling the pain and let me see if I can investigate it more closely with my testing.

(I am monitoring the patient with my hands in an FCT testing position—neutral—as I'm giving him the instructions. When his mind shifts to the painful area, he goes into stress. Now you have two choices: If you're very familiar with the anatomy of the shoulder, you can begin to mentally sift through the locations and types of tissues very systematically. Until you have obtained this level of knowledge and organization, you can also prepare a list of the relevant locations and tissues. Prior to doing this, you can also remove the test filters in your FCT kit from their typical storage sites and place them in a convenient order and location. The current stress response will be matched when the correct location or tissue is identified, and there may be more than one. You can determine which is most significant and what is secondary (a consequence of the primary stress).

Depending on your knowledge, skill, practice, and innate ability (gifts), you will do this with FCT filters, written lists (use of pictures works, too), or your mind. If you're uncertain, you will probably also need to use a method of checking your work. There are several:

A. If you did use FCT filters to identify the problem, the patient is likely to have little or no stress response to nearby filters (unless there is another problem or a cascade of troubles from the primary trouble).

B. Use a global vial—I like to call it an umbrella vial (a vial that covers many different related concepts, areas, tissues, or pathogens)—that contains the information for many different musculoskeletal and nervous system aspects relevant to the shoulder. First, place the suspected problem filter on the plate and adopt a neutral testing position. Then, place your relevant shoulder area umbrella filter on the platform. If you were correct, the patient will not go into stress. In other words, what you have identified has captured the most relevant structure concerning the local aspect of the pain complaint. (This technique is useful in many ways that I will also discuss later.)

C. *Remove all vials from the platform. Tell the patient or speak silently with a statement (not a question) of the answer: "The pain is coming from the shoulder joint." If you are correct, the patient will remain in a neutral position. If you are wrong, you will know immediately. If you were incorrect, it is most likely due to inaccuracy caused by a testing error that might include the possibility an assumption about what the problem was because of what you thought or what the patient told you. In other words, you just were going through the exercise of testing to prove your hypothesis, not discover the cause. It is also possible that you did not have an accurate answer because you lacked the mental software, a complete list from which to investigate, or the possibility that there is no FCT vial that represents the patient's problem. The patient also may have been unclear and not as helpful as was intended.*

D. *Make it more real, as I mentioned before. Stop the testing and muscle test around the finding. If you know your anatomy, localize a good spot with your hand. If you have the filter, use the filter. There are plenty of ways to do this, and like anything having to do with FCT, you get better with the right intent, knowledge, and experience...Or is that frequent flier miles of the never-ending traveler?*

Now back to our patient.

Yours truly: I think the pain is coming from the shoulder joint itself, not the muscles or attachments. I could be wrong, but that's where I'm picking up the greatest stress. I'm going to see if I can figure out why it's become so much worse this year. If we can find out why, then maybe we can do something to get you better besides the Florida vial...Boy, I sure wish I had one of those vials!

(Depending on the patient's response and how well I know the patient, this might be a time to make it more real or continue testing with the intent of identifying some treatable factor[s] that are affecting the shoulder joint, and likely other joints and regions, too.)

Patient: I like the Florida idea, too, but it would be nice to have that shoulder not bother me so much.

Yours truly: Just relax. You might as well relax since you're lying on the table. If I were you, I wouldn't even think about shoveling at the moment.

(This kind of test and description is to illustrate the main ideas in this section of the book. I would not describe it as a comprehensive test, but it is a good example of meeting the patient where he is at. Having said that, I will tell you that there is more than one way to go about the next step. Let me share a couple of them.

A. *Use your FCT filters to hunt for a match or matches to the shoulder joint filter. Think in big categories first and test with master filters such as various toxicities, infections, iatrogenic factors, nutritional deficiency, physical trauma, and so on.*

B. *Use your knowledge, in whatever form you learned it, of shoulder problems to query in big categories such as these mentioned or others that you have discovered through your own experience and study. Perhaps your software is upgraded because you are a nurse, physical therapist, massage therapist, chiropractor, acupuncturist, or serious student of anatomy and physiology and acquired it through study. Perhaps your software has been upgraded by testing many other patients with shoulder complaints, so you have some ideas of what might be at the root of the problem.*

Your testing is complete and identifies that the shoulder joint is affected by tick-borne illness and dietary factors. There is also physical trauma to the joint. Use any of the methods mentioned previously if you need to reinforce your findings. Depending on the findings and the response of the patient, you might want to help make it more real for him. Complete your testing by focusing the rest of the test on what is needed to support the patient to clear the influence of tick-borne illness. Test further to identify the dietary factors, especially those that relate to the purpose of his visit.

Yours truly: I'm sure there is some wear and tear on your shoulder, but according to my testing, the joint is being bothered by a tick bite.

Patient: I got bit last year and went to my doctor. He gave me an antibiotic and said that would take care of it. I didn't remember about that until you brought it up. How did you figure that out?

Yours truly: Your body told on you, and it says that one of the reasons your shoulder is giving you more trouble is the tick bite, even though you took the antibiotic. Let me show you something that you might find kind of interesting.

(This would be a good place for you to bring out your dog named A and your pony named K. If this is the first time the patient experiences this, I would make sure to add a couple of steps so the response to the tick-borne pathogen(s) and some other irrelevant infection (something he does not have) can be contrasted. I would localize to the shoulder joint, too. Again, there are lots of ways to do this, and your skills and the situation with the patient will determine the how, the when, and the if. Your dog and pony have learned a lot of tricks and put on quite a show. After the muscle test demonstration, I move on.)

Yours truly: Often when I see evidence of a tick bite, I will find there have been a lot of things that change. You might not connect it to the bite, but I'm wondering if you feel more tired and not as sharp mentally—maybe a little foggy.

Patient: I do, but I guess I figured it was just about getting older—like the arthritis.

Yours truly: Maybe you're right, but if I'm right, besides your shoulder hopefully getting better, you will feel more energetic and less foggy.

Patient: That would be great.

Yours truly: I'm going to make some remedies for you to help your body get rid of any remaining influence from the tick bite. I think this is the main thing that has changed in the past year. *(This statement can be tested too, right?)* I noticed that there are some other things besides wear and tear that were affecting your shoulder and other parts of you before the bite. You've probably just become used to them.

Patient: What do you mean?

Yours truly: I suspect that you have an old injury or trauma to your shoulder, which is why it is a place that speaks loudly when you use it to shovel snow. *(We might discuss an old athletic injury, a surgery, an accident or fall, or a physically demanding job.)* I also think that your diet affects your joints, including your shoulder.

Patient: I've always eaten about the same.

Yours truly: I think that potatoes and grains containing gluten, like wheat, rye, and barley, are inflammatory for you and that one of the places affected is your joints.

Patient: You want me to change my diet? No potatoes, no bread, no beer? What am I supposed to eat?

Yours truly: You don't have to change anything you don't want to. All I'm saying is that you might feel better if you did, including your joints. This is the part of the process that many people don't want to hear about, because it might involve changing your lifestyle. Like I said, you don't have to change anything, but I think that if you cut out these foods for a month, it would be plenty of time to see if you feel better—joints, stomach, bowels, energy level, mood…You might be amazed by how much we're affected by what we eat. I would just like you to consider it. *(Again, I might muscle test around some of these findings and localize to digestive locations or joints besides the shoulder. I might two point with the food or use contrasting responses with stressful versus non-stressful foods. It depends on the particulars of each testing situation.)*

Yours truly: After you're done with your schedule, you can let me know if you've tried anything with your diet. We'll see if the tick-borne trouble still shows up and what the level of stress is like with your shoulder joint, and you can tell me how you're feeling.

Patient: Thanks a lot.

Yours truly: I'm really glad that you came in, and I think good things will happen.

Patient Helps You to Specify the Factors

Now, wasn't that fun? The previous example can be applied to many situations when the patient comes in with a complaint that he or she thinks is coming from a certain organ, muscle, etc. I think that engaging the patients as I just described helps you in your efforts and helps them to trust in the testing process.

Another variant is working with the patient to identify relevant factors to explain a symptom or illness. In this example, the patient comes in to see you with a respiratory complaint.

Patient: Thanks for seeing me. I have this cough, and it's not getting better. It's going into my chest. I'm not sleeping well.

Yours truly: Let's see if we can figure this out and get you back to feeling better. Why don't you lie down on the table and I'll test you?

(Put your hands in a neutral position after having established testability/reliability. The focus is on determining what factor[s] is responsible for the cough.)

Yours truly: How long have you had the cough? (*Cough is in your mind—the patient changes to a stress response.*) One week? Two weeks? (*Stress response is still showing.)*

Patient: I think about three weeks. (*Stress response is still showing.*) No, maybe a month. (*Stress response disappears.)*

Yours truly: Where were you a month ago?

Patient: I was visiting my mother in Florida.

Yours truly: How did you feel when you were there?

Patient: I don't really remember. Maybe I started coming down with something then. (*If you're tracking the responses, you will sense when her recollection has identified what you're focused on.*)

Yours truly: I think you were exposed to something when you were down there, and you're still having a hard time with it.

Patient: Like what?

Yours truly: Let's try to find out.

(Here, you have many options. Here's one way that is again done mentally, with filters, or with additional helps as previously described. Do your intending in silence or out loud with simple statements, phrases, or words. Infection, toxicity, chemical sensitivity, allergens…you're monitoring all the responses from the driver's seat of your FCT car.)

Yours truly: Where does your mother live in Florida?

Patient: She lives in a retirement community in her own home.

Yours truly: How was she feeling? Was she sick?

Patient: Well, she has had a cough for many years and uses an inhaler. She has plenty of health problems.

Yours truly: I would like you to try something. I want you to think about your mother and put her in your mind. Let me know when you've got her. (*You have her mother's cough in your mind, and a stress response is measured. Mold matches with some allergy responses, and yes, I just introduced another topic to be discussed later.*) I'm pretty sure that one of the reasons your cough has not disappeared is mold, and maybe that is one of your mother's problems, too. It could be in her home; when you're down there for several days, you get a big dose of it

Patient: It's very damp down there. I also don't like a lot of the air fresheners she uses to cover the musty smell. I've wondered if I might also be sensitive to some of the flowers down there, too. *(You are monitoring all of these pathogenic factors to determine relevancy as she describes them. She has helped you to identify the origins of her problem, and now it is time to fix them. Determine also if there is a current, non-Floridian challenge that is affecting her ability to recover.)*

Yours truly: Have you been taking anything to try to help with your symptoms?

Patient: I tried two different antibiotics, prednisone, and some essential oils. I thought it actually made me worse. *(Remember, you're monitoring for relevancy.)*

Yours truly: Which antibiotics and essential oils?

Patient: Amoxicillin, then Azithromycin. I also used peppermint and eucalyptus oil. (*Your monitoring identified Amoxicillin and peppermint oil as complicating factors)*

Yours truly: When did you stop using them?

Patient: I was done with the Amoxicillin a couple weeks ago and took the peppermint and eucalyptus oil yesterday.

Yours truly: I think that the problem started with the mold, but you're also being affected by the Amoxicillin and the peppermint oil.

(Depending on the patient's responses to your answers, you can decide if you want to do anything to make things more real. Complete your testing so that any other relevant filters can be identified to support clearing of the mold(s), allergen(s), and peppermint oil. Identify through your testing which pathogenic influence is affecting which organs/tissues., and ask which organs/tissues require a supportive remedy. Many organs may be affected, but all of them may not require support. Why guess when you can test? This is one of my mottos—the patients hear it a lot when they wonder and speculate about what's bothering them. In this instance, there could be other present factors besides iatrogenic effects that are interfering with recovery. It is possible. Again, why guess when you can test?)

Back to our patient.

Yours truly: I'm going to give you remedies to treat these three things in the order your body asks for them and the support that is needed to help you recover.

Patient: I hope this works.

Yours truly: Me too!

Patient Helps You to Specify the Timing

The previous example gives you many ideas about how you might use your investigative skills to cooperate with the patient and uncover which factors are responsible for a particular problem. Your limit is your own imagination and the ability of the patient to work with you to explore various events. Sometimes there is a clue in the patient's history, sometimes in the conversation with the patient prior to testing, and sometimes during a conversation during the testing process (which is the basis for sharing the previous example), during which a memory of some kind will be triggered. The value and accuracy of the memory to the particular problem can be assessed "online" during the process of testing. This information can lead to further downloading of memories and further evaluation of the coherency of the information to the present task.

You can go great distances in time and space (the non-local qualities of consciousness) with this technique as long as you have an open mind and learn how to keep your ego out of the way. I say this as a challenge to any dowsing rod enthusiast, pendulum user, and, yes, ankle holder, too! This does not mean we should run away from the use of devices or the focused intent that are essential when it comes to the investigation of those experiences and theories that are grouped under terms such as mental radiesthesia, but it's just a term. Let it also be said, dear reader, that patients can be highly suggestible to the pet theories of a practitioner or someone who is held in high regard by them. Therefore, one must find a way to surrender positionalities and favorite agendas to receive information of high quality. Just as importantly, those of us who have our tools, toys, and methods for accessing potentially useful information are not immune from the same pitfalls. I will say more about this in the last section of the book.

Patient Helps You to Specify a Place

The example in the previous section is intended to highlight the value of timing and situational factors, again with invaluable assistance from the patient. In this next case, your testing has identified that radon exposure is a significant problem.

(You have been busy doing some initial testing, or "mapping," and according to your findings, you will be addressing the effects of radon exposure in your treatment.)

Yours truly: According to my testing, exposure to radon is having a significant effect on your health. I think there are connections to several organs, including your thyroid, parathyroid, lungs, bones, and bone marrow, so I want to look at this more closely.

Patient: Really? Nobody has ever told me that. Where's it coming from?

Yours truly: Let's see if we can try to figure that out. It could be that your radon exposure has come from one or more of the places you've lived. Let's try something. (*Put the radon filter on the platform. The patient will go into stress.)* I want you to think about your current home. Imagine that you're back home right now and sitting in your living room, okay? Can you do that?

Patient: Sure.

Yours truly: Let me know when you're there.

Patient: I'm there. *(The patient has stayed in stress mode.)*

Yours truly: Where did you live before that?

(The patient answers, and we continue this process of her visualizing herself in each of her previous homes, all the way back to her place of birth, checking for responses with each. To finish our example, we skip ahead to her place of birth.)

Yours truly: Where were you born?

Patient: I was born in a small town south of Milwaukee called X. *(As the patient thinks it—indeed, before she can even state the town name—the patient goes to neutral mode. Remember, you know this. Why? You're in the car.)*

Yours truly: I think that's where your radon exposure came from. How many years did you live there?

Patient: I lived there until I left for college.

Yours truly: Where was your bedroom?

Patient: In the basement.

Yours truly: Do you have any siblings?

Patient: Two sisters.

Yours truly: How's their health?

Patient: They have lots of complaints, too, that are similar to mine. We all have thyroid problems *(and so on and so on).*

Yours truly: The effects of radon exposure stay with you, even if you've not lived in homes that had high radon levels since your childhood, so I'm going to treat you for stresses related to radon. I have a baseline from my testing showing how strong this influence is. When you come back after the treatment, we can compare these numbers and see if you're feeling better, okay?

Patient: That sounds great. I always wondered if there was something that wasn't right about the house I grew up in. I never slept very well, and I felt anxious a lot. I felt better when I left home.

Yours truly: That's very interesting. Maybe there was some part of you that knew the environment wasn't very healthy. It will be fun to retest you and talk with you after you've finished your schedule.

Patient: I'm looking forward to doing this and to feeling better. It really helps to have some answers about why I feel this way. Do you think I will get better?

Yours truly: I don't know. I don't make any promises, but I can tell from the testing that radon exposure is a very powerful influence on your health. I think it should have a very positive effect!

Dear reader, are you having any fun yet? Salivating? Rediscovering your love for travel?

The Experience of Near Misses and Almost, but Not Quite

What does a phrase like this mean in this context? When searching for an answer, the match for what is affecting a tissue or organ, I have thought about several scenarios. Is there one key pathogenic factor or several waiting to be discovered? These questions and comments are my way of encouraging you to reflect upon the idea of a near miss, resulting in an almost, but incomplete result. Dear reader, use my comments as an invitation to formulate your own interpretation. To get things going, consider this: Did you know that the patient's responses will move ever closer to a match with each letter, each syllable, and each word that approximates the answer, finding the mole in hiding? Dear reader, did you also know that when you offer a different menu of alternatives, the "body" (by now you must know it isn't really the body) will give you the correct answer or direction? (Do I go left or right at the next intersection?) I invite you to try this for yourself! It's very possible to make a wrong turn and be in the right neighborhood, but at the wrong house.

I offer a silly metaphor to emphasize what I consider to be a very important point: You are in the energy field or country that we shall call Lungland. What is disturbing the residents of Lungland? Who are they? Why are they there? Intelligence has informed you that it is the M tribe, and you have evidence to support the fact that this is good intel—still, it is not enough to save Lungland from the threat. You send your forces out, telling them that you need more information to be able to do anything constructive, and more intelligence comes back that it is a fringe group (a new mafia?) called the Micopeez. You are grateful for the additional information, because it has allowed you to triangulate their position.

You are ready to intercede and save Lungland and its inhabitants, and you order a strike, to be delivered in a little bottle that contains the answer (remedy). You wait for news and are told that there was a temporary calm in Lungland, but a short time later you hear that the problems have not gone away. More investigation eventually uncovers that the force behind this unrest is a splinter group from Micopeez called MicopeezUltra, and this is the cell that directs all the operations. This time, when you dispatch your forces, there is a powerful conflict, but a lasting peace. All is well in Lungland and for its inhabitants.

The moral of the story is that you might be fooled or mistaken by a match with a closely related pathogen, at least on an energetic basis, because of a close relationship. You made some contact with the target, but not the bull's-eye. As I alluded to, you can count it down to the last letter, maybe even to the inflection of each syllable. (Yes, I really do mean that.) There are more targets, more moles, than one can probably fathom. Do you think every mole is in your kit, your notes, or your software? How would you know the difference between a mycobacterium and a mycoplasma? How good is your aim and intel? How would you know the difference between *mycoplasma pneumoniae* and *mycoplasma hyorhinis* by a syllable or by a filter? What if you didn't possess the filter? What if you didn't know about all of the other moles? Am I reaching you? Dear reader, am I getting through to you?

If you don't have a filter for it, is it in your software? If it's in your software, what are you going to do about it? (More about this will follow.) Could your near misses be interpreted as matches because the conclusion to the story is driven by your need to find the match? Could it be because of your belief that the match is in your kit or is discernible in the algorithm? Dear reader, while this section in the book is brief in length, it is very important. Do not be fooled! I have spent many hours on this topic. Presumably, it will eventually move you, and hopefully forward you on your one-way trip!

Finding the Bull's-Eye

Dear reader, I am trying to at least encourage you to think about what to consider when you thought your moves should have resolved the problem, but didn't. (*I know I did it right…I did the protocol. The patient should be better. Maybe I missed something. Oh, that's right, there are more layers.*) I vaguely remember the details of a discussion about five years ago with an FCT expert who knew way more about FCT than I did at the time. The answer to my question was that the remedy would be close enough, a good near miss. Maybe I was missing something.

Those are the kinds of answers that engage my personality and its quirks. Not satisfied, I started doing my own hunting for bull's-eyes, and I would not share these comments with you if my hunting did not find rewards. I will try to illustrate this with three examples concerning *borrelia*, mycoplasma, and mold. If what I've said in this section hasn't led you to consider that you might be missing the bull's-eye every once in a while, then you might want to ignore the rest of this section...and probably the rest of the book.

There are plenty of examples to choose from. Let's try tick-borne illness, for starters. Are you certain that you know every pathogen carried by a tick? If you are, I wish I could say that I always shared your confidence. Let's say that your testing has led you to the conclusion that tick-borne illness is the problem—you found the matches in your tick-borne illnesses arsenal of FCT remedies. However, the patient is not nearly as improved as you expected after treatment, and there is still stress in some of the best hiding places, such as the meninges or cerebrospinal fluid. You might discover another pathogen that you did not expect to find there. Maybe you obtain (or develop) an additional vial for *borrelia burgdorferi* that produces a response from the patient even though there is no longer any response to the *borrelia*-related vials in your kit. I have had these experiences when treating tick-borne illness...I think I might have just tripped the heresy alarm.

Mycoplasma is another interesting example. Over one hundred different types of mycoplasmas have been identified that affect other various species. I think there are approximately twenty types identified in human tissue. How many kinds of mycoplasma vials are in your kit? Do you think there might be others that would be significant? Would you know to look for them or to consider them in your thinking if you only believed that any mycoplasmas of significance were already available to you? Do you see what I'm suggesting? You can only look for what you have and what you know about. Awareness of other possibilities, or at least being open to other possibilities in your testing, will open doors. I have had some interesting results with vials for other mycoplasmas, including *hyorhinis*, *hominis*, *arthritidis*, *genitalium*, *pirum*, *penetrans*, *haemofelis*, *salivarium*, and *fermentans*. Hitting a bull's-eye in this way has uncovered new findings for several patients. Will somebody please turn off that alarm?

These mycoplasmas have connections to varied problems, including cancer, arthritis, periodontal disease, skin problems, and pelvic problems. Providing these remedies has helped patients when other closely related remedies (near misses) have done little or nothing. According to my testing, there are interesting connections or associations with other pathogenic factors when various mycoplasmas are present. Obviously, each finding raises more questions and opportunities to learn—one of the beauties of FCT!

One last example: The fungus known as *Coccidioides*. It's not in your kit. Do you know what it is? How would you know about it? Why would it be relevant unless it was part of your mental software? Again, do you see what I mean? I discovered its importance by asking new questions. I developed my own questions and my own algorithms about fungal infection because so many of my patients were farmers. Through this same process, I had previously expanded my collection of fungi outside of the FCT kits to include fungi that I knew were likely problems for residents of the Midwest who spent time outside: Farmers, gardeners, hikers, athletes, kids, etc. I also expanded my collection of mycotoxins produced by these fungi. These steps allowed me to uncover other pernicious agents that were affecting my patients. I also collected many samples from barns, chicken coops, farmer's fields, gardens, woods, basements, and so on. (More about this in a later section.) However, it did not occur to me at first (because of the limitations of my own thought processes and context) that the molds that were bothering so many of my patients might be coming from somewhere besides the Midwest.

I developed an H vial for mycoses, and it was exciting to me (but should not be surprising to you by this stage of the book) that I found a number of instances of eliminating the stress to the highly expanded collection of molds and seeing that these toxins did not eliminate all of the stress to mycotic infection. The reason has now become obvious—a no-brainer—to me. I was clueless about these deficits until I expanded my thinking. What if the source of the molds was from outside the Midwest? What if

I had not considered them in my thinking? What if I did not possess them? This led me to develop filters for *Coccidioides posadasii* and *Coccidioides immitis*, both very important molds in the southwestern United States and certain arid regions of Mexico, Central America, and South America. By now, you can probably guess, dear reader, what happened. I was able to find these molds in many of my patients, who had lived or traveled to these destinations and picked up the spores.

Several patients improved markedly with the administration of these remedies. I was able to identify through testing and with the patient's confirmation the state or country in which the infection took place, and I made it real for the patient by identifying not only the place, but the time the infection took place. I made it more real in some situations using the dogs and the ponies. I correlated the findings to the symptoms, which included not only respiratory and sinus complaints, but in some instances, other very significant disturbances: Joint, neurological, and emotional problems. I added to my mental software by reading many of the papers published by the Valley Fever Center for Excellence at the University of Arizona. These ventures into the world of *Coccidioides* opened my mind to other relevant aspects of my patient's histories, including the life of a Midwestern snowbird who vacations in places like Arizona, a traveler to Mexico who wasn't ever quite the same after his return, and an avid hiker back from an exciting week of hiking in Nevada.

I hope these three examples open up your mind or at least stimulate your salivary glands. These examples illustrate a point that I say at least once a day in my clinic: I'm smart enough to know that I know just a little bit. This is why I'm trying to offer you some of my strategies. This way, you can find out things for yourself and potentially help another person because you operated with an open mind. Carry your humility and your curiosity with you so that you can be open to new findings and not just repeat a very good but, in my opinion, very limited algorithm. When someone struggles and I'm not able to help them, I ask God to keep sending me to new destinations.

I offer some additional ideas to help keep you from near misses, but with no guarantee of bull's-eyes, either. Why? I just shared with you that you might not know what the bull's-eye might be or where to look for it!

Here are some starters for you to play with: Your mind (intention) could begin with, *There are one, two, three pathogenic factors.* What did that tell you? I've already alluded to how you can derive your number. Here's another: Use your FCT filters that have generated your matches (or near misses, or almosts, but not quites). Then give it the white-glove test with a confirmatory match that you have created for the same problem. As I mentioned in an example, does your *borrelia burgdorferi* vial find no other stress after you have offered all that you can from your FCT filters?

Trust your testing to give you the answer. You might assume that all of the relevant information was already provided by the other filters, and if that is the case, the patient's problems will surely disappear, right? What if the problems don't go away? Will you blame yourself? Will you think you missed something? I hope these comments will help you to go a little easier on yourself and encourage you to do your own out-of-the-box thinking. I am hoping that you might think differently about this with a little encouragement from yours truly. Now you know better and are potentially a little smarter, a little wiser, and a lot more humble about how little you really do know.

CHAPTER THREE

Applications to Concepts with Relevance to Toxicology

This selection will include significant portions of a lecture that I gave in 2012 to a group of FCT students. The feedback from the lecture was very positive, so I thought it would be useful to include it in the book. At a later date, several of the students who attended the lecture also came to my clinic to observe my work, receive encouragement and training while they tested patients, and ask questions about my strategies and theory.

I want to try to illustrate my thought processes around the application of FCT to disturbances caused by toxin overload instead of having you try to memorize or record specific protocols that I have used to treat various patients affected by toxic exposures. I will try to give you some specific ideas about how you can further investigate potential patient exposures to toxins with some methods and relevant questions to ask your patients that I have developed to, I think, help you become a better detective when investigating how toxins might be a significant part of the many different kinds of symptoms and diseases that affect patients.

Albert Einstein once said, "Not everything that counts can be counted and not everything that can be counted counts." I'm hoping at least some of what I can count counts for something, and I recognize that I haven't counted everything that counts—not even close! I've been emphasizing this point from the very beginning and will continue to do so.

Dear reader, as you can tell by now, interesting findings frequently lead me to new questions for exploration that would be intriguing to study in my spare time. I think this is probably similar to what Dr. Yurkovsky has often said about FCT being an incomparable tool for investigation. However, I think that it is also true (as I believe he has also often stated) that while many findings are quite interesting, it does not necessarily follow that all findings appear to be as important or meaningful when it comes to improving the health of the patient. I think that's another way of paraphrasing Einstein's quote. I'm not much for military analogies, but I think you have heard plenty within FCT about high-value targets, and I am using my terminology to express a similar thought. While we are concerned with treating what is most relevant to help our patients, we expect that those in conventional medicine are seeking to do the same. Conventional medicine tests generate an almost endless list of findings, but do not necessarily establish their clinical importance. Einstein is right.

I think about this issue frequently when my patients come to me with their lab reports. There is so much fear or relief that is connected to the belief systems about a particular number. Have you ever met someone whose first name is Bell and last name is Curve? There are also many belief systems under the surname Effect with the first name of Cause. Yes, their middle initials are A. It seems to me that there is a big difference between saying "A causes B" and observing that there are multiple imbalances or disturbances that are reflected in many tissues that include A and B, but also C and D and many more—this comment is applicable to conventional medicine and all of its counterparts, as well. Applying this thinking to FCT might generate the following: Perhaps in a subsequent FCT test after taking some remedies, stressful responses are no longer detectable in the testing regarding C and D. This is interesting, but does this mean that the treatment proves a causal relationship between the remedies doing something to C and D, or was it more circumstantial? Was it the reflection of some other changes in the adjustment of certain homeostatic mechanisms that are now reflected in a different status about C and D? What is the framework for interpretation of the findings, and does it have sufficient explanatory power?

Monocausal linear thinking is potentially just as big a problem in FCT as it is in conventional medicine. My thinking about toxicology, my ideas around FCT testing and treatment, and my personal context for understanding what is taking place in the process of testing continues to evolve, and I suspect that this might be the case for anyone if she approaches FCT with an open and curious mind. Consider thyself, dear reader. You will read this book and reflect upon the merits of FCT with a certain background or education and experience that shape your perspectives about what FCT might be able to do to help you expand your ideas about health. When you begin doing FCT, not unlike undergoing any other new learning, you will probably start slowly and tentatively, trying to exactly copy the protocols so as not to make any mistakes and arrive at the best possible answers and treatments. This is the place you need to begin. You might stay there or venture into other places, and as you can tell, I implore you to venture.

In my own circumstances, I spent many hours studying Dr. Yurkovsky's tapes, e-letters, articles in the *Townsend Journal*, and book and spent hours testing my family and friends and deepening my understanding of bioresonance testing and various energetic modalities through other sources. I tried to blend my training in biochemistry, toxicology, and traditional Chinese medicine with FCT. With practice, with prayerful intention, and with God's help, my skills grew and good things happened. If you think about your FCT findings, I believe you will also find yourself continuing to ask questions about your tests and patient outcomes. You will continue to study and be a lifelong student. You will make interesting discoveries, which may lead you to try new things, develop new methods, and expand your context to better explain your findings. This is what has happened for me, and I am trying to share it with you.

In this section we consider these entry points from the standpoint of applying them to toxicology. Remember what I said about entry points and the associative principle of mathematics? As with any other focus, your mental software will shape your inquiries into the topic of toxicology. For example, if you understand that the cell is the basic unit of life, you will be asking questions and looking for answers that fit into these ideas. Alternatively, if your context is based on some other fundamental ideas about energy, quantum physics, and the extracellular matrix, you might have a different perspective and understanding about the cell's importance relative to its environment. You might have a different appreciation for the effects of toxicity and its targets instead of a pharmacological or toxicological one. The more you appreciate the differences between biochemical tests and bioresonance testing, the more inclined you might be to look for a different context to understand health and the effects of all kinds of toxins (environmental pollutants, of course, but also EMFs, medications, bacteria, viruses, food additives, negative emotions, and so on). What I'm trying to emphasize is that your own intentions, educational background, experiences, and context cannot be separated from your practice of FCT.

Many of my current ideas regarding intracellular and extracellular communication in the connective tissue matrix, as well as some of the homeostatic mechanisms that are activated in response to noxious stimuli, are influenced by Dr. William Rea, Dr. Mae-Won Ho, and Dr. Alfred Pischinger. Their writings appeal to me because in many ways, they represent some kind of synthesis, a larger context than my earlier training in biochemistry and toxicology. To again use the image of mental software, I am always working on additional software enhancements or upgrades to expand the context for interpreting my FCT findings. I encourage you to do the same using these and other sources. I would encourage you to become familiar with the works of these authors and see if you find them to be helpful.

Yes, this updating is a never-ending, ongoing process—I think you catch my drift about being a perpetual student. I think FCT testing requires it of you! I believe it makes me a better FCT practitioner and a better person. Your questions, thoughtfully asked, provide answers—and, of course, more questions. FCT could not move forward without the knowledge acquired through testing and the evaluation of responses to treatment. These answers need to fit into a larger contextual framework that brings everything together and enables you to provide even better results through even better questions! If you simply test people mechanically, doing the same thing over and over again without thinking about your findings and the results, you will not develop your mental software.

Key Concepts

I don't think we can begin to talk about FCT and toxicology without first sharing a few ideas about homeostasis and the lack or loss of it, dyshomeostasis. Human beings are remarkably designed to carry about the processes of homeostasis. Homeostasis is reflected both in coherency and in the lack of it—an equally important concept, incoherency.

The more that we are able to grasp the significance of the structures and processes that operate in a healthy person, the more we will be able to understand the consequences of toxic exposures to those structures and processes. Our context for understanding how these structures and processes are involved helps us understand which filters will most likely be affected and not be surprised by finding stress to those areas identified through the testing. The more we understand the many aspects of homeostasis, the more, I believe, we would wish to have many, many more filters to investigate the details of the structures and the mechanisms operative within all of the individual homeostatic subunits that must function seamlessly together for a healthy response. In my vocabulary, this seamlessness is another word for energetic coherence. More filters and more information are helpful not only from the standpoint of important pathogenic factors, as discussed previously, but also regarding the identification of structures that help us to cope with toxins and the stress that is produced.

Let's begin by talking briefly about energetic coherence. We are highly coherent beings, and stress in any form produces incoherence. I say "any form" because negative thoughts and destructive agendas also produce incoherence, both within ourselves and non-locally. Toxicity in any form, including EMFs, introduces incoherence into the body. Incoherence obscures light, including the Light of our Source, and interferes with function. I think this is a very important topic, and it is not one just for the physicists. Yes, dear reader, we are trying to expand the context for toxicity and health. In the broadest sense, toxicity has connections not only with physical incoherency, but emotional, mental, and spiritual incoherency, as well.

I am grateful to many great people for their work, but especially to Dr. David Hawkins for his conceptions about coherency, harmony, and truth. Again, I commend his writings to you. Yes, his are very important shoulders for me to stand upon! Incoherency has many consequences on both a microcosmic and macrocosmic level, and the loss of coherency between tester and testee will affect your ability to test accurately. I have already made mention of this difficulty. From a physical standpoint, on a cellular level, a lack of coherency spells inefficiency and energy loss. I think that incoherency can be used as a component of a big-picture context for thinking about various biochemical processes, including ATP production and energy utilization, from a biophysical point of view, so for now I'm just throwing out some ideas about the application of concepts regarding coherency to many important topics, which you can explore on your own. I think that FCT is a tool to help identify some of these incoherencies and potentially provide the proper input to correct them. Here, our focus is on the consequences of exposure to toxins. As always, it is important to talk about the value of reinforcing coherence in our testing, our subliminal questions, our thought processes, and our intentions for the patient.

I would like you to think in terms of seamless communication, or a highly organized, coherent energy field within the body that is instantaneous and utilizes virtually no energy. This requires the expansion of the models that have been in place to understand toxic exposure, but more importantly, to redefine health. One source for my appreciation for new models comes from those researchers who have lifted up the importance of water and its ability to receive, store, and transfer information.

I would suggest that your appreciation of this broader context of the importance of water from a structural and biophysical perspective would be enhanced by reading Dr. Mae-Won Ho's writings. The unusual properties of water combined with those of the proteoglycans, glycosaminoglygans, glycocalyx, and connective tissue proteins are responsible for the creation of a highly flexible, intricate, and dynamic system that functions like a liquid crystalline matrix. (Much has been written by others about the remarkable properties of water and its ability to hold and transfer information, to have memory. I encourage you to read authors like Dr. Bill Tiller, Dr. Cyril Smith, and Dr. Masuru Emoto for further software upgrades about this subject.) This living watery system allows for storage of coherent energy. Any subtle influence anywhere within the system is quickly being shared throughout the system, and this system is able to hold information and respond to new information. Amazing! Dear reader, be amazed each time you receive or make a homeopathic remedy and struggle to explain to others, or yourself, how it really works!

When the highly ordered matrix in your body becomes disorganized or less coherent, there is a loss in energetic efficiency and greater susceptibility to disease, and the breakdown might be attributable to a toxin and its effect upon a certain organ. I think it is also useful to think about how the toxin may have introduced a breakdown in communication, a loss of information, or the introduction of new information, not unlike a virus on your computer. The instructions for the operating system have been invaded, your software doesn't run as efficiently as it used to, and so on. Another good book to help with your physical conception of the matrix and the importance of the system as a whole for the maintenance of good health is *The Extracellular Matrix and Ground Regulation* by Pischinger. Again, consider it an appetizer and an invitation for your own investigations, dear reader! There are plenty of shoulders for us to stand upon.

Thinking through these concepts energetically as well as biochemically, thinking about the body's response to toxicity as a whole organism versus a single system, thinking about the importance of the matrix versus the cell (just the opposite focus from that of my formal training), and thinking about the ideas of informational or vibrational medicine versus pharmacological models are some of the aspects that shape my testing and interpretation and are now a part of what I referred to earlier as my mental software. We are estimated to have 100 trillion cells in the entire body, with the highest number of cells being red blood cells, which are numbered at around 35 million. That's a very big and highly coherent communication network. How does that compare to T-Mobile or Verizon? While there are many different kinds of cells, they do share the same basic characteristics regarding the mechanisms of cellular respiration and elimination of end products. This is important because every cell releases its products into the connective tissue matrix, which is our common communication network. The connective tissue matrix receives information almost instantaneously when any type of cell has been damaged or destroyed by toxins. This initiates a compensatory, global, homeostatic response. The almost liquid crystalline matrix is the hub of information reception and distribution through the body regarding any toxic exposure that affects its coherence. When you are testing someone with FCT tools, you are running your own scans of the other person's software that will reflect these compensatory mechanisms, and all in the name of maintaining as much coherency as the system can maintain under the circumstances. (Yes, I know it's just a metaphor.)

Even when considered from the limited context of being only a physical frame of reference, the system is probably too complex to fully comprehend. The scientists who are materialists certainly have their work cut out for them. If you consider the system from a non-material perspective, the almost endless numbers of players in the matrix are organized and responding to a non-physical boss called consciousness. The influence and control of the nuts and bolts of this matrix is affected by other realms or aspects of our being, and many of them can be influenced or directed by intention. My testing and treatment supports this way of thinking. Dr. Bill Tiller's intention experiments and model are available for reading, and there are many others who have written about how the physical and the non-physical, or the scientific and the spiritual, find a higher synthesis in consciousness. Pick *a* century of writers, your favorite continent, or your favorite religious or spiritual tradition and read for the rest of your life.

The complexity of organization in the physical realm is not the whole story, but it is amazing and I think that you will benefit by reading about its features. For example, consider how this extracellular fluid is continually being circulated throughout the body. It contains nutrients and ions that are required for cellular life and is under the control of what Pischinger calls the ground regulation system, which consists of many structural proteins that together form the connective tissue networks that are part of the information distribution and storage system. Yes, all of it is linked to the remarkable properties of living water. Despite the specialized functions within each person and the necessary hierarchies of function and communication, as physical structures (and non-physical system, too), we are amazingly able to operate as a whole. When toxins affect a specific organ or tissue, it is recognized by the whole person regardless of where the problem got its start. In this sense, the response to toxicity will always be the same whether or not there has been a local, regional, or central injury, either physical or non-physical. Receptors that exist locally in the skin, the mucous membranes, and the connective tissue matrix perceive and transmit entry information into the body, and the responses that follow are highly coherent. I wonder where all of the other receptors are hiding, like when someone gets under my skin or I think about Ardith—my wife, my sweetheart, my Valentine—and I can't find the goose bump receptor, only the evidence of one further down the line!

Highly coherent responses mean that we are ideally suited to respond only to the extent that is required; for example, for some toxins, we give just a local response to conserve resources and minimize the disturbance. When there is excessive, persistent exposure to toxins that cannot be handled locally, there will be more obvious regional and centralized responses. This constitutes a more costly form of containment and a greater use of resources to maintain as much coherency as possible—it is one thing to be cut off in traffic and another to be disowned by a loved one. It is one thing to be outside when the wind is coming from an uncharacteristic direction and brings the aromas of the nearby sewage treatment plant and another living every day in a moldy house. Toxins in any form create incoherency and chaos. If the toxic exposures are powerful and enduring, there will be injury and a loss of vitality. Incorrect information will create stress. There will be damage, physical and non-physical, to software and hardware. The loss of parts of the communication system will isolate certain physical structures or limit the ability of these parts to work harmoniously with others. There will also be the damage to non-physical structures, the informational fields, the subtle energy structures, and so on. (I don't want to restate or re-spin the many models that have been well described elsewhere concerning subtle anatomy) The result is separation and the experience of limitation. This kind of description makes more sense to us when we think not only about cells and tissues, but the extracellular matrix, the importance of water, and the loss of coherency through toxic exposures. Do you know that you can evaluate this for yourself through your testing and develop your own theory or conceptualization about these phenomena? By now, I hope I have at least encouraged you to think that you can.

You have many filters in your test kits that you can check for stress caused by exposure and injury to toxins. Build your mental software by studying what is known about how different types of toxins and how their patterns of exposure affects the patient and her symptoms. Ask lots of questions. Be a detective to help her uncover when and where these exposures took place. Consider the non-physical toxins, too, for these are no less real than living over radon-contaminated soil. *Feelings Buried Alive* by Carol Truman is another valuable book to introduce you to the idea that toxins come in many forms. Yes, more shoulders! Consult the authors I have already mentioned to determine the significance of toxic stress to certain organs or tissues so that you can correlate your findings with your expanding knowledge of how the body is affected by toxicity. Otherwise, you may only be a mechanical tester. This way, when a patient asks you what a hypothalamus is, your response will not make you sound like a testicle!

As you test more and more people, you will recognize patterns of toxicity, making it easier to uncover the origins by asking more relevant questions of the patient and knowing where it might be best to look among your filters for help. The stress to the patient may seem to be coming from everywhere, but you need to find its true source. One more time: As Albert Einstein once said, "Not everything that counts can be counted and not everything that can be counted counts." That about sums it up, doesn't it, dear reader?

Big-Picture Questions and Considerations to Investigate Toxic Exposures

This brings me to what I will refer to as big-picture considerations about toxic exposures.

Big Picture Point #1. A broad vision is required that can help to make sense of particular observations about patients and FCT findings. If you are in the middle of the forest and you have no clue where you are, it is helpful to have a compass, and one might say that the degenerative and stress organ filters in FCT test kits provide such a compass. Is there more required besides these fifteen filters to make your way out of the forest? How does the identification of the most stressed organ help you make sense of the effects of toxic exposures? What is it that you're actually measuring? I keep repeating my point of view about this topic because I think it is so important. If there are nagging themes in this book, this one has to be at the top of your list.

Big Picture Point #2. We will need to distinguish between acute and chronic responses to toxic exposure. This consideration raises many relevant questions that I find are reflected in the test results, but the significance of the findings is not always so obvious. Here is what I mean by lots of questions: How long ago did the exposure take place? Was it a single large exposure or was it a long-lasting low-dose exposure? Is the exposure still going on? If the exposure has stopped, how long ago did it stop? Does the exposure involve more than one noxious stimulus or incitant? If there is more than one stimulus, are there antagonistic or synergistic effects? Are there differences between patients who are exposed to the same toxins (for example, they live in the same town or are part of the same family or work in the same job)? When there are differences (but your testing identifies the same incitants), how do you understand the differences? Is an acute response experienced equally throughout the body? Can some aspects of the patient's current condition be understood as responding in an acute fashion while other tissues or organs or systems are responding in a chronic way…all at the same time?

See? I warned you. There are lots of relevant questions. Asking good questions of the patient and learning about their symptoms is of some help, but it will not tell you the answers to most of these questions, so how will you interpret your findings to answer them? How can you tell if the protocol you write will be able to take the differences and priorities between acute and toxic exposure into account?

Big Picture Point #3. We will need to distinguish between homeostatic and dyshomeostatic responses to toxins, which also brings up a number of questions and interesting observations that have been made about the varying responses to external stimuli. Dear reader, prepare for another blizzard of questions: Can you distinguish between a healthy and an unhealthy response to a stimulus? Is the response linear (a direct relationship between dose and response)? Is that a functional or dysfunctional response? Is it a threshold response (in other words, the patient appeared to have no problems until they reached a certain level of toxicity), all of a sudden bringing some negative response? Is that a sign of health or a lack of health? Can your FCT testing tell the difference? Is it a hermetic response (perhaps like a homeopathic or extremely low-dose stimulus, the initial response benefits the person, but after a particular dose is exceeded, the response becomes increasingly negative)? Is that a sign of health or a lack of health? Can your FCT testing and your context for understanding the body's responses to noxious stimuli make sense of this? Can you tell if you're dealing with an acute or chronic problem?

Big Picture Point #4: We will need to distinguish between local, regional, and centralized responses to toxins. What do I mean by this? Do the degenerative and stress organ filters help you to understand if the response that you are measuring is primarily local, regional, central, or all of the above? Why is this important? Can a patient recover her health, or is it more realistic to say that the current compromised level of health may be helped from further decline?

Let me add a few more ideas about the level at which the body is engaged in responding to toxicity. The body seeks to maintain homeostasis with as little expenditure of energy as possible. Moreover, the body is a thermodynamically open system. In other words, it has no choice but to continually respond to every stimulus, internal or external. Open systems exchange energy and matter with their surroundings. This should also encourage us to consider that the human responses to toxic exposures involve multidimensional relationships, including synergistic responses, in which the whole is much more than the sum of its parts and cannot be understood by reducing the whole to its parts. It is more than singular cause-and-effect responses. Linear causal thinking, which characterizes much conventional thinking and medicine, will be inadequate to explain or appreciate homeostasis once we expand our thinking about information reception, storage, and response in an open system.

For example, most conventional thinking continues to see the cell as the primary functional unit of the body. This has been, for the most part, such a highly accepted and unexamined given, or dogma, that it is an example of what I mean by a limiting context. The cell is not the whole story. If the basic tissue or basic unit of the human body is the extracellular matrix, not the cell, we might think very differently about our findings. If we thought that the extracellular matrix was only a reflection of a higher level of coherency coming from a non-physical source, then what? Oh, that isn't science? That means it is unimportant? That means it cannot be tested? Dr. David Hawkins frequently comments in his books that the answer to a problem could come from a higher level of consciousness or a more expansive context.

Why do we expect that our answers to questions about toxicity will find a final answer in the materials of the cell or the matrix? Dear reader, I'm just asking. Homeostasis is not a fixed point, but a dynamic equilibrium that represents a continual effort of each system to remain within an acceptable range of function, so if a human being is exposed to some particular noxious stimulant, all of the necessary tools are designed to be available at the local level through the connective tissue matrix to handle the stimulus as long as it isn't too large or too long and there are sufficient resources (such as an adequate nutrient pool) to take care of it. Obviously, if there has been prior damage in the local environment, this ability will be compromised. Other answers may emerge if we expand the model beyond a physical conceptualization of homeostasis and to a context of coherency that includes physical, emotional, mental, and spiritual domains within consciousness.

Let's go back, for the moment, to the physical side of things with this discussion: If the body is unable to handle the problem locally, it is addressed regionally. Other tissues or organs or spinal segments or "whatevers" unbeknownst to us may become involved. If matters cannot be handled at this level, there will be centralized involvement. Through the connective tissue matrix and the subtle anatomy, there is two-way communication going on all the time at all levels and at nearly instantaneous speeds. Because of this, I think there are even more questions that one might be asking. *Uh-oh*. Here comes another blizzard of questions: When your patient is lying on the table and you are conducting the test, what level of response are you measuring—local, regional, central? This triggers additional questions, doesn't it? (I know what you're thinking: *You and your darn questions. You're off to break another record.*)

Yes, here we go again: How can you be of more help to the patient if you are able to determine the level of response? Could one filter be reflecting a local response, another a regional response, and still another a central response? Could one filter be reflecting a combined response coming from all levels? More importantly, how is the level of response related to the various reasons the patient had for coming to see you? How much of the response is physical, emotional, mental, or spiritual? Does the level of involvement give you information about the prospects for improvement through FCT remedies or any other modality? Is the stress that you are finding in a particular filter coming from an alarm response, an adapted response, a periodic disturbance, a long-standing aperiodic disturbance, inflammation, tissue damage, tumors, or necrosis?

Questions, questions, and more questions. We might also ask if the fifteen different filters all speak about the same problem or if they reflect a mixture of problems. Do all of the degenerative organ and stressed organ filters speak in unison about the same type of homeostatic or dyshomeostatic response or the same type of stress? By now, dear reader, I must sound like a broken record. Perhaps you are getting to the point where you would like to break one. I just don't know when to quit, do I?

Practical Examples of the Big-Picture Questions

Let me give you a simple but practical example: Your patient comes for testing in the middle of the morning. She ate breakfast two hours ago. You are doing your testing and find that degenerative organ 3 is SI Mucosa. You determine that SI Mucosa is being affected by food intolerance/sensitivity. It is your first balance to this filter. It does not test as a food allergy, but there is a stressful response to food. You ask her about what she had to eat, and she tells you that she ate fruit and had coffee with cream. You determine through testing that she has a stressful response to fructose and to lactose. (Incidentally, because in this case it is a food intolerance response and not a food allergy response, there may not be a balance to the food allergy vial in the test kit, and you might not have thought about this unless I mentioned it, right? Let's hear it for every little software upgrade! You may have to obtain some other vials to determine this, although I will tell you that this information is available through subliminal testing, as well.)

You investigate further and find that not only her SI, but her LI, lymphatic vessels, and other structures are stressed by her breakfast. Perhaps you ask her how she's feeling, and she tells you that she feels a little bloated, but it's not that big a deal because it's not really preventing her from doing what she needs to. What are your findings telling you? I believe what you are measuring is an alarm response to the food, which in this case is probably the most recent incitant. I find that this response can be measured for at least four hours, and sometimes longer. This is the body's "normal" response to some kind of stress.

Perhaps there are reasons that can be uncovered in FCT testing for her particular sensitivity to these substances. You could do her a big favor by encouraging her to avoid them. If she can't part with her fruit and coffee for breakfast, at least you might be able to help her handle it better by suggesting she take digestive enzymes with her meals. I find that this is generally helpful for not only indigestion, but generalized inflammation as long as there is no evidence of ulceration of the GI tract. You would also do her a favor by encouraging her to harmonize all her food and drink with a Food MEMON prior to consumption, which would eliminate the negative information in the food that is probably generated through not only food additives and pollutants, but also the processes of food preparation. It's interesting and makes you feel good that you can help her in so many ways.

My main reason for bringing this example up is pointing out that her body was in an alarm state at the time of testing, which is the reason the SI Mucosa filter appeared where it did in the testing. I believe that if she had been tested four hours later, she would have tested very differently. Therefore, I generally ask my patients if they have eaten recently; if they have, I will look for evidence of an alarm reaction. If they show for such evidence, I will try to identify the sources and take the level of stress for those affected organs into account so that I can factor them out and distinguish those responses from other issues. I also typically find that those structures that are affected by food sensitivities also have other periodic disturbances or aperiodic disturbances. There may be inflammation and tissue damage, and these structures may be nutritionally depleted, as well.

There is another interesting aspect to this example: When these exposures have taken place over a period of time, it is common for there to be an experience sometimes referred to as "spreading," which means that while initially the body had a powerful negative response to some incitant, it now responds more globally to other related incitants, as well as to smaller doses. The person has become hypersensitive. The patient might say, "I used to be able to eat anything [that is an indication, by the way, of an adapted or masked response], but now I don't know what I can eat." There are many factors that contribute to the single measurement you make that indicates there is stress in a particular organ. What is the actual nature of the stress? How can you tell? Questions, questions, and more questions! (*If he uses that Q word one more time, I'm gonna…*)

The Last of the Big-Picture Questions…Maybe

The single measurement obtained from a filter for any organ, tissue, nerve, etc. is a functional measurement. It tells us something of the functional state of that structure, and I'm pretty darn sure that something is far from everything. How does your testing help you to understand its functional state? (Yes, dear reader, one more time, another front of questions is coming in.) Is it adequate to say that it is stressed? Is it sufficient to identify a pernicious influence that balances the organ and, through splitting, identify others? Does an indication of stress to a particular filter provide sufficient information to make these distinctions? How do we take into account the timing of the treatment? Can we split the contributing factors that make up the particular functional capacity of a particular structure through subliminal testing? When we assess the patient's responses to an FCT treatment in a follow-up test, can we not only determine if we have perhaps eliminated the stress from a particular toxin, but can we also assess the overall status regarding the functional capacity of the patient? Is the patient more able to handle new exposures? Have the guidelines for avoiding certain triggers helped the patient reduce the overall total body load of pollutants? Can we tell if the person is more nutritionally and energetically equipped to handle noxious stimuli at a local level? Is there evidence of reduced inflammation? Is there less triggering of symptoms by low-level, diverse stimuli, and can we help them understand why that is the case? If there is additional greater sensitivity to incitants (a common occurrence that may be linked to alterations in the number of receptors), can we explain why this is not necessarily a sign of poorer health, but a sign of progress?

These are my big-picture considerations with some of the questions (some *questions? Are you kidding me?* Some *questions?*) and considerations that are currently integral to my testing and interpretation of findings. My goal is to continue to analyze my work in the clinic with these kinds of questions in mind and to pose them in the course of testing. Hopefully this analysis will provide new information and potentially expand the context of your thinking, too, as well as your posing of questions and the answers that follow, and ultimately lead to a better model to help patients deal with our toxic environment.

Not All Responses to Toxins Are the Same

Not all responses to toxins are the same. There are big-picture considerations and concepts concerning homeostatic control, which help to explain the particular responses of patients. The main ideas that I use to understand my test results come from other scientists and my earlier training in biochemistry and toxicology. I have organized this part of the book as it relates to the information gathering, storage, and transfer functions of the ground regulation system and the principles of how the body adjusts itself to toxicity according to homeostatic mechanisms. In my opinion, the following principles are very useful:

First of all, we need to always keep in mind the total environmental pollutant load, a concept that can be applied not only to physical toxins. There will be some point in any person at which there is present significant noxious stimuli to generate a response. The type of response will depend on the properties of the stimuli (half-life, virulence, and interaction with other stimuli, as well as metabolites) and several other parameters. If the person enjoys a high state of health, there will be a short-lived stress response to the stimulus while the body eliminates the problem that is known as an alarm state. Decreasing the total environmental pollutant load, whatever the source (biological, chemical, EMFs, emotional, mental), through avoidance and elimination of the stimuli itself and through the body's mechanisms for recovery will help to explain some patient responses. Alarm responses indicate that the body not only has the capacity to respond efficiently, powerfully, and appropriately, but provides the patient and the healthcare provider with a much easier prospect for identifying the source.

Secondly, hypersensitivity to some stimuli *or* an apparent lack of responsiveness to stimuli can be related not only to the total environmental load, the kind of stimuli, and the varied responses to stimuli (linear, threshold, or hermetic), but also to how long the body has been suffering under a heavy burden of toxicity that exceeds the total environmental pollutant load that it can handle, resulting in either temporary or potentially permanent changes that have taken place. There is diminished function, but in other instances, there will be exaggerated responses resulting in an increased sensitivity to stimuli. These diminished responses could also partly be attributed to a diminishing supply of nutrients and a lack of or misuse of non-physical resources!

We can perhaps explain some of the patient responses as examples of adaptation. (Can you see Selye's shoulders from where you are?) In these situations, the consequences of pollutant overload over a period of time have affected homeostatic control both directly and indirectly, and this represents a more significant problem. At this level there will be direct damage and deregulation of blood vessels, possibly evidenced by inflammation, spasm, edema, plaque, and so on, and the immune system will be directly involved in responding to the threat. Mechanisms to remove toxins and dead cells and repair mechanisms will be activated through the ground regulation system. There will be indirect, negative effects on homeostatic control evidenced by endocrine and immune dysfunction and especially autonomic nervous system dysregulation. This stage of adaptation is the point at which it becomes difficult to identify the pollutant sources because the causes are masked; in other words, the body becomes used to the exposure...Thank goodness for our little tools to help us.

This, of course, does not mean that everything is just dandy, because although the body was able to neutralize the problem, accommodations have been made. This comes at the high cost of increased energy demands and eventually early damage. There may be various symptoms such as fatigue or pain, but the cause and effect relationship between toxicity and these symptoms has been masked or lost through adaptation. This is often a significant part of the clinical picture with patients who come for FCT. Again, the picture becomes more complex when the non-physical domains are included.

Another important principle to consider is that the patient's responses are highly individualized and dependent on the innate abilities of that patient. It appears that despite significant pernicious influences in their environment, some people enjoy substantial resilience and maintain a relatively high level of homeostatic control. A different person's world seems to crumble with the slightest insult. When two people are exposed to the same toxins at work, their symptoms and severity of response may be different. It could be that innate, genetic resources may afford a higher level of resistance or susceptibility to toxins for some people. We must also recognize the existence of biochemical individuality of response and emotional constitution and guiding belief systems. The individualized response of one person may be further differentiated from someone else due to the activation of genetic resources through individually different epigenetic pathways that are not only affected by genes, but the relationship between genes and the environment. The response may be further refined by who that person knows, how she interacts with others, and so on.

Another example of a highly individualized response is described by a principle called bipolarity. This could mean that initially, the patient might feel good after response to some stimulus; once the stimulus is removed, however, the patient may experience an overcompensation from the stimulus and feel tired, depressed, or maybe hung over. If this pattern occurs repeatedly in someone who has passed the alarm phase and is in an adapted state, this may eventually cause exhaustion and the appearance of some diseased state. Hypersensitive patients with chemical sensitivities eventually lose these periodic responses. If the loss of hypersensitivity has not taken place because the environment load has diminished but because of the progression to an aperiodic state, we know that the body is on a degenerative path that is heading toward more serious illness. You may hear of these different responses to pollutants from your patients. Listen to their stories to get your clues and sense of direction.

Sometimes patients will tell you that over time, they have become more and more sensitive to an increasing list of incitants, and they also tell you that it takes a smaller stimulus to bother them. This, too, is a sign of pollutant overload and an indication that dyshomeostasis is occurring locally, regionally, and probably centrally, as well. While the responses are still periodic, the longer these exposures take place, the more likely it is that there will be more serious health issues.

Here is a third important principle: When these exposures continue past the adaptive phase because of pollutant overload, when the higher energy demands have simply become more than can be handled, or when there are insufficient nutritional resources, the patient will eventually reach the stage of exhaustion with tissue breakdown and various fixed-name diseases. Many of your patients will fall in this category. Perhaps many of them have functioned well in a masked or adapted state for many years and have therefore ignored or failed to recognize the continued significant exposure to various pollutants until one day they were diagnosed with a serious illness. This is a common experience in our toxic environment that goes unrecognized due to an aperiodic presentation with eventual end-stage disease that seems to all of a sudden show up one day. Listen to your patients' stories for evidence of this pattern.

These kinds of patients are the most difficult to help because they remind me of my limitations and who is really in charge. Your work with them may exert its greatest influence on other planes than the physical one. It may extend to their loved ones. Their serious illnesses may afford us the chance to work not only them, but the chance to work on ourselves.

Applying Toxicity Concepts to Patients

Let us begin with a straightforward case to see if we can both understand the value of the testing and find explanatory power in these concepts and principles in order to help the patient and better understand what has been taking place. I chose these real life situations from the clinic to try to illustrate what I think are some important variables to explain key differences in the responses of patients to pollutants and other noxious stimuli. We will save the discussion of non-physical toxins for the last sections of the book.

A Boy and His Allergies

A mother brings her adolescent son into the clinic for treatment of his "allergies." His symptoms are runny nose, itchy eyes, post-nasal drip, and congestion. He was treated with several different over-the-counter antihistamines with little effect. The mother asks me if I can fix his allergies, and I ask, "How do you know it's allergies?" (I think she probably thought I was ignorant and clueless.) I test the boy, and the testing indicates that there is some sensitivity to grass and weeds, but the most important stress (which I now often refer to as acute factors) is the presence of chemical toxins, specifically high levels of lawn chemicals. I ask the boy about his allergies, and he tells me that he never had issues with allergies until this summer, when he got a part-time job cutting the lawns of many of his neighbors. Most likely, the majority of his customers treated their yards with various lawn chemicals, and the symptoms got worse as the summer progressed.

According to FCT testing, his olfactory nerve, the olfactory lobe, and hypothalamus are highly stressed to these chemicals, causing autonomic disturbance. I find that if there is chemical sensitization of these structures, there is heightened response to other incitants like grasses and weeds. His troubles are resolved not by treating him for allergies, but through an FCT protocol for eliminating the influence of lawn chemicals and remedies for the stress created in his autonomic nervous system. What else can be said about this case? Actually, quite a bit.

The boy did not have any other significant health complaints according to his mother or the patient history form. The allergy trouble did not begin right away, but got worse as the summer wore on. Apparently, he had minimal or no symptoms at first. I think this suggests that the exposures were relatively small and that his systems for detoxification of lawn chemicals were functioning reasonably well.

Perhaps his symptoms began as a result of the accumulation of greater and greater amounts of chemicals until he reached a threshold that started to bother him. Since we are open systems that must respond to all stimuli, there were undoubtedly other types of exposures, including the allergens from grasses and weeds that led to the onset of symptoms. Perhaps the onset of symptoms was also related to an increase in the number of summer jobs, meaning that the actual amount of exposure was also increasing. Perhaps there was a particular lawn on which the owner used excessively large amounts of chemicals. Perhaps the onset of symptoms was also attributable to a diet that failed to provide his system with adequate amounts of certain nutrients such as Vitamins B2, B3, and B6; Fe; Zn; Mg; Se; Cu; Vitamin C; phosphatidyl choline and bioflavonoids; and adequate amounts of oxygen so that the cytochrome system for detoxification of pollutants could operate at maximum efficiency.

Perhaps if he had made it through the rest of the summer and not come to see me, a good number of his symptoms would have lessened or disappeared with his return to school and the removal of the noxious stimuli; his body would have had a chance to catch up, resulting in reduction in total pollutant body load. Perhaps if that had been the case and he returned to his summer job the following year, he would have experienced similar troubles but with an earlier onset of symptoms if the body remained affected by the previous summer's exposure to toxic chemicals. Perhaps the test results would have been very different if his mother had taken him first for conventional treatment and he was given medication. There are a lot of "perhapses"…I thought you might prefer this to the overused Q word from the last few pages.

The boy had a good response and a short course of FCT treatment because of his overall good health and relatively short term of exposure, and he didn't wind up in the hospital or ER because the level of exposure was relatively small and, though frequent, not continuous. The disappearance of symptoms through the FCT treatment indicated overall good health with the ability to respond to the remedies. I think this case is a good illustration of the fact that the elimination of the influence of toxic chemicals instead of an allergy treatment would help his system to work better so that it could return to a healthier state. His responses to incitants were periodic. In other words, there was a stressful response that was followed by a return to his original or nearly original state. (His symptoms disappeared when he wasn't mowing lawns.) However, there was also some adaptation in that the autonomic nervous system held some imbalance, which was identified by FCT testing, even after the stressful exposure stopped. He did not report symptoms of diminished or exaggerated sense of smell from the lawn chemicals.

The presence of stress in the olfactory nerve, olfactory lobe, and hypothalamus filters indicated that the information from the airborne exposure affected not only the local environment of the nasal mucosa, but also the regional environments of the sinuses, the tonsils, and so on and the central regulating centers of the autonomic nervous system. We might also ask ourselves how else we can be of help to this patient. If the boy returns to his summer job next year, he can be encouraged to minimize his pollutant exposure by cutting lawns several days after the chemical applications by his customers, and he is more likely to do that than wear a mask. What kid is going to push a lawnmower in front of his friends while wearing a mask? I also find that if there is some susceptibility to airborne allergens like grass and weeds, there is great benefit to taking a remedy prior to exposure for grass or weeds.

Breathing Troubles

A mother brought her son into the clinic with breathing problems. His tonsils were swollen, he was anxious, and he complained that his head hurt. His mother told me that she took him to the ER the day before for extreme respiratory distress. The mother said that he was given antibiotics and steroids and sent home, so apparently there was enough improvement to send him home. He was told to come back for a recheck the next day to see if the tonsils were still swollen. If so, they recommended surgery—a tonsillectomy. I tested him and found no evidence of infection. FCT testing identified acute factors of a chemical origin that had nothing to do with infection, the reason that antibiotics were given. The testing indicated that he was acutely stressed from exposure to formaldehyde, VOCs, and fire-retardant chemicals. His smooth muscle, bronchioles, capillaries, and several structures in the brain stem were among the most-stressed tissues.

Here's where the detective work comes in: Sometimes it takes a little bit of digging, because the mother isn't thinking about toxicity from an unidentified environmental source. She's been told that it must be an infection, so her context for thinking about what's happened to her son has been shaped by the ER doctors. (Be careful: You might be likely to also accept the same context or batch of facts—A caused B, and then it was C.) She's likely to think that maybe they didn't get the right bacteria, or maybe it's a virus. Maybe they gave her son the wrong medication. Eventually my questions led us to determine that the boy's symptoms began after a new carpet was installed in the basement, including the bedrooms of her two children—one day before the trip to the ER. The mother told me that her son liked the feeling of the carpet, in contrast to his sister in the adjacent bedroom. He slept on the floor, directly on the newly installed carpet. His sister did not sleep on the floor. This explains why he became so ill and she didn't.

I made remedies for him for the chemicals being released from the new carpet, padding, and adhesive. He made a quick recovery. His swollen tonsils returned to normal, so he got to keep them!

Let me share a few more comments about this case. The difference between the first case, with the lawn chemicals, and this case, with the new carpet, is the dosage and ongoing exposure. In the case with the new carpet, the threshold of exposure that could be contained by local or regional resources was quickly surpassed. The other important difference is the difference in the type of toxin. The carpet and carpet-pad chemicals are able to easily pass through the blood brain barrier, and obviously, all chemicals are not of equal virulence for many different reasons.

The boy's symptoms improved after leaving the bedroom for the ER, but began to return when he returned to his room. I advised his mother to ventilate the room well and have him not sleep in the room for several days. How can we help to determine when it will be a safer environment? Obviously, if the boy returns to his room and there is no return of any symptoms, it is safer. There is another practical thing that you can do, which has many useful applications when it comes to environmental toxicity. This leads me to a related subject that you can add to your software.

What Can't You Make a Remedy From?

I think you can probably make a remedy from almost anything—okay, everything. When I suspect that someone is being affected by toxins at home, at work, or outside, I give them instructions to help collect samples for testing. These test samples can be made into test filters and, if necessary, into remedies. Let me give you several examples, including this case:

In the last example, I told the mother to place a bowl of water in the room, something that has a good amount of surface area. Leave the bowl out overnight and then transfer some of the water into a small glass jar and bring that water sample to the clinic. If there is a significant amount of chemicals still present in the air, a small amount of them will be found in the water sample through FCT testing. If the sample shows for new carpet related chemicals, use the sample to make a test vial. Typically, I do this at 30X. Alternatively, or in addition to this, a very tiny sample of the carpet and carpet pad (perhaps from the corner of a closet) could be removed and brought to the clinic for similar testing. Once the treatment of the boy is complete, the 30X test vial can be used to see if there is any residual stress from the chemicals. If so, the test vial can be used to make a treatment vial at the appropriate potency. This method of determining whether a particular environment is still a problem includes an additional benefit: The chemicals found in the air of the bedroom or the fibers of the carpet are more precisely identified in the collected sample than the existing filters in an FCT kit. This allows for a better match and better results.

If you are uncertain after concluding a treatment for chemical toxicity as to whether or not all of the key toxins have been eliminated and are no longer creating stress, you can always express this concern in the form of a subliminal question or by searching the existing filters for various kinds of chemical toxicity. It also needs to be said that with tens of thousands of different toxins in our environment, we would need enough test kits to fill an entire building to have an inventory that began to approximate their numbers. Therefore, sample collection is often invaluable. While it is true that there are certain key toxins like mercury that can be added to the kit, it is also true that in an open system, every toxin contributes to the total body load and may trigger reactions, even though all toxins have their own individual properties and virulence. The interactions of toxins with other toxins add another layer of complexity to the identification of all toxic materials. This is made even more complex because the most important toxicological effects might be from the different metabolites that are produced by non-enzymatic and enzymatic processes of oxidation, reduction, and ligation, and not the original toxin.

Other useful sample collections include outside samples for environmental chemicals, molds, and allergens. In this case, we instruct our patients to leave a bowl of water out on a dry, windy day for twenty-four hours. You will acquire a good sample of what is currently in the air near their residence that might be causing stress in this time. Outside samples placed in yards, on decks, in barns, and so on provide a wealth of information and a very good treatment tool.

There is also much that can be learned by collecting inside samples. Here are a few examples: A patient who worked in a manufacturing plant and had headache and respiratory complaints was greatly benefitted by collecting a sample from work and using it as part of the treatment. He had no idea of all of the chemicals in the air and told me the company kept a MSDS (Material Safety Data Sheets) book with hundreds of pages, which meant hundreds of chemicals. Instead of trying to identify all of the possible toxins from the MSDS book, a sample was collected, a test vial was prepared for testing (which also provided a way to measure the loss of the stress to the chemicals), and the creation of remedies was made to the matching potency based on the testing.

Here's another example of how to do this: A man who worked in a business where he was frequently preparing resins for repairing windshields complained of debilitating headaches, brain fog, neuralgia, and skin rash. In his case, we collected samples a little bit differently. We mixed resins together in the clinic just as he prepared them at work (actually, outside in the parking lot) and collected the gas that was generated from the chemical reaction into clean vials from which we made test filters and eventually remedies.

One more example of how and why to do this, and another interesting case in which sample collection was invaluable: A school teacher with varied complaints attributed her symptoms to a toxic classroom. She also told me that many of her students do not feel well in her classroom. When she was home for the weekend, she would slowly start to feel better again, only to return to school and feel worse. She tested very strongly for mold, solvents, and VOCs. She had complained to administration and was told that her room had been tested and it was fine. What did we do? We used the method I have just described to you.

I sent her home with three empty vials: One for her classroom, one for her bedroom, and one for her basement. She put bowls of water in each location for a day and then transferred a sample of each into the vials. When I tested the vials, the samples from her home were clean (as I like to say, boring), but the sample from the classroom showed mold (*Stachybotrys*), solvents, and VOCs. The testing confirmed her suspicions, but because she had no recourse except to quit her job, she took a Classroom Isode every day after work, which alleviated her symptoms.

Let me give another example of a different type of indoor isode: This man was a welder, and in the past few years, he used an electronic welder. He tested very strongly for EMF sensitivity from many different sources, including home and work. I gave him an empty vial filled with MEMON-harmonized water and told him to keep the vial on his person while he was working for an entire week. I was interested in the contribution coming only from his workplace, so I had him keep the vial wrapped in aluminum foil when he left work and take the foil off when he was at work. When he came in with the vial and we tested it, it was very high in EMF. I used it to make a Workplace EMF Isode, which he took every day after work. This greatly helped his headaches, brain fog, energy, and mood.

One final comment regarding sample collection from inside or outside sources: Anything can be tested, and if necessary, a remedy can be prepared. This includes substances like the lotions, creams, soaps, essential oils, cologne, deodorants, and makeup people use. It includes the various kinds of food given to pets or livestock. It includes the chemicals sprayed in yards or gardens and on house plants. It includes the water from the well, the filter in the furnace, and the supplements being consumed. Use your imagination! Sometimes I think it is very helpful, although time intensive, for my patients to bring in suspected stressful substances for testing. This might include foods, makeup and other skin products, well water, hay, or cleaning materials. You can make a remedy from anything, though, so I hope this is a helpful tip. You will need to add on to your clinic space to find a place for them all!

Heart Palpitations

A semi-retired man in his sixties has unpredictable, intermittent heart palpitations. He says that sometimes his heart seems to skip a beat. He is understandably nervous about the condition of his heart. However, when he leaves home for several days on a camping trip with his son, his symptoms disappear after a couple of days. What a relief! When he returns home, his symptoms return. After being home for a couple of weeks, the symptoms are occurring daily and with greater intensity. What is going on? Once again, it is time to play detective. Our conversation eventually identifies that for the past few weeks, when he's been home; he's been out working in the barn, sawing up logs for lumber. What is the condition of the logs? He tells me there is lots of mold on them. I ask him if he wears a mask. I think you already know the answer.

FCT testing identifies that he has very high stresses to mold. Giving him remedies for mold and the affected organs and giving him the necessary information to protect himself eliminates the problem. Incidentally, if I was uncertain about the identity of the incitant(s) because of a lack of a close match in the test kits, I could have sent him back to his barn and the moldy logs and told him to collect a sample, as previously described. The sample would be used for testing and potentially treatment, but in this instance, that was not required. Again, this is an example of a periodic stress to the patient that is based on the level of exposure to the incitant—in this case mold—in which a good result is obtained. Avoiding moldy environments during his recovery will decrease the likelihood of being susceptible to symptom aggravation from other moldy sources.

I will compare these cases, which are easily reversible, with others and try to offer some explanations for the differences. Let us summarize some common aspects about these particular cases and connect them with some general toxicological principles and the responses of the patient to maintain or regain homeostasis, first. The overall level of pollution from all sources and the body's specific and non-specific responses to these stresses does not appear to have left lasting damage in the form of tissue damage or a particular disease. Apparently, the patients had adequate resources to handle the incitants. In other words, they had a sufficient pool of nutrients to allow the many subsystems to work efficiently.

The withdrawal of the stimuli quickly improved the patients' health. Returning to the environments that contained the noxious stimuli aggravated the patients' health. This observation not only points out the effect of the total body load of pollutants, but also demonstrates the capacity to deal with toxicity in the form of periodic responses. The periodic responses represent higher levels of health than aperiodic responses, in which there is no obvious response from a patient to increasing levels of toxicity. Alarm reactions are not negative, but tell us that the patients have not lost the ability to respond to environmental stressors. It is true that each stress depletes the body of energy, but the lack of a response would tell us that there has previously been a series of non-adaptive or maladaptive responses to stress. If this had taken place, we might expect to see with the withdrawal of the stimuli some return to normal function, but with some losses of function or chronic symptoms. In other words, the patients would exhibit signs of decreased energy and eventually signs of deteriorating health until many periodic responses were no longer evident. This is not a good path, for it is the journey not only to maladaptation, but eventually to exhaustion and end-stage disease. When a particular system, organ, or tissue reaches this stage, I don't think that there is much we can do, even with a tool as powerful as FCT.

Perhaps the most important point to be made thus far is the high value that can be placed upon detective work, or identifying the type of exposures and their sources, which will undermine the patients' health. Treating the patients for these exposures and educating them about the significance of these exposures so that they can be reduced or eliminated at the earliest stage possible is the best course. Sometimes equipping them with the necessary nutrients, at least in the short term and done best through diet, but potentially also through supplementation, may help to minimize the damage and conserve energy.

These kinds of cases are interesting, and success, in terms of highly favorable patient outcomes, is very high. When there has been no damage or relatively little damage, it is only logical to expect full or nearly full recovery of functionality. I see many patients who fit into these categories. However, the most challenging patients do not fit these criteria, and we will spend the rest of our case study time discussing these cases. These patients may have so much damage from toxins that many tissues and organs are beyond the point of recovery without a miracle. In some of these instances, the goal will be to identify the source of the damage and try to halt the deterioration. When you are trying to help people in this situation, it is very difficult. Illness offers both the patient and the practitioner the chance to grow spiritually.

More Complexity and Greater Challenges

While many of the patients who come to the clinic have relatively easy complaints to turn around, the majority of my patients have aperiodic disturbances, long-standing inflammation, and tissue damage. I am not even close, in most cases, to being the first person to see them about their problem or problems, so when they are tested for the first time, it is also a kind of a movie, or a record of the effect of at least some of the treatments they have or are currently receiving. You must keep in mind that when it comes to toxicity, our bodies use the same means to detoxify everything, whether it is an environmental pollutant, a medication, an antibiotic, an herb, a vitamin, or some other supplement. It's not like we have one liver for the pollutants and one for the medication and one for the food. It all gets taken care of by the same incredible organ.

Each of these so-called helpful substances is potentially an incitant, as well. While the treatments are intended, of course, to help the patient, they may have inadvertently compounded his or her problems and added to the total body burden. The treatments may have damaged the immune system or the ground regulating system or contributed to the imbalance of the internal environment of various organisms, including so-called friendly guests. In some instances, the goal of the treatment might have actually been to suppress certain systems and subsystems, including the immune system, to discourage inflammatory responses. (You know you're in for trouble when the patient shows up with a grocery bag full of supplements or more medications than can be listed on your intake form!) The patient may have received numerous courses of antibiotics and steroids, which have left their signature on the patient. You can find this out in the testing process, and through the remedies, you can initiate a tremendous improvement in their health by treating them with isodes for the antibiotics, steroids, and other medications. These patients frequently come with non-physical toxins, too—tremendous emotional stress and limiting belief systems about their health that do not exactly do them any favors. You might even test to see if the illness or the belief systems around the illness are the main problem. This, too, can be investigated. No, I'm not kidding.

What do you do when the patient asks you if you can help him? How long will it take? How many sessions will he need to pay for? My standard and less-than-satisfying answer to some patients is that I don't know, and it will depend on many factors that will be determined as we go through the testing process. I inform them that not only will the testing identify where we must focus the treatment, but it will also determine the order of treatment, the strength of the treatment, and the treatment intervals. There is no other way. You must test them and try to determine the impact of their history of treatments on their current level of health. Can you spell iatrogenic? Are your patients obsessed with a disease name, a bad number, or a lab report? You might have to treat them to relieve them from the effects of their prior treatments before you can address the underlying problems. There are additional difficulties if the patient is continuing to see other providers, because their interventions may be at cross purposes with your own and add further to the toxic burden and energy demands that are being placed upon the patient.

This reminds me of a case in which a woman saw a doctor who treated her with a combination of oral and IV antibiotics for over eleven years. I wonder if that is a record. She told me that she really didn't get any better, but she wasn't too much worse. It took several months to treat her for what I would call the toxicity or incompatibility of the antibiotics to her overall health before her body was ready to actually treat the underlying tick-borne illness. The initial FCT treatment protocols eliminated long-standing digestive complaints and strengthened her immune system, as evidenced by a lack of colds and respiratory complaints that had also become chronic.

I have also had several experiences with patients who developed various troubles after vaccinations. In one instance, a man felt "off" (dizzy, brain fog, sore joints, stomach troubles, disturbed sleep) shortly after receiving a flu shot. I asked him to obtain information from the manufacturer about the specifics of his flu shot, and he sent me the specifics from the pharmaceutical company that listed all of the ingredients of the vaccine. He was sensitive to several substances, including formaldehyde, thimerosal, and polysorbate 80. I sent him home with remedies for these chemicals and organ support identified through FCT testing, giving him only what his body asked for. I saw him a few weeks later. He told me that he completed the schedule and had felt increasingly better as he made his way through the schedule of remedies. Do your own detective work about what goes into a vaccine. What you learn may be of great use to someone—maybe not to every single person, but it will only take one of the many for you to be glad that you did.

This example illustrates a very common situation that you will encounter, because many of your patients will be on medications or will have received other treatments, including vaccinations. In many situations, my patients have been able to eliminate all medications, but not because I told them to (you have to be careful that you do not say anything that would infer you are giving conventional medical advice or that you are practicing medicine without a license). What I do tell them is to monitor how they are doing, because if the root causes for the homeostatic disturbance have been accurately identified and treated, the person will be overmedicated. For example, if your patient is on blood pressure medication and you are giving him remedies that may correct the causes of his elevated blood pressure, tell him to monitor his blood pressure. One other bit of practical advice is to encourage him to talk about his medications with the pharmacist. Never give instructions about medications, medical tests, or treatments that would indicate that you are in charge of any of it. Make sure that you explain to every patient that FCT is not a medical treatment or a substitute for it. Reinforce what you say about this subject with written statements for the patient to read and sign. Despite these attempts to be very clear, there have still been times when I have been misunderstood. Be kind. Be careful.

More Thoughts about Complexity and Adaptation

Let's think about the idea of adaptation first, because it is always a component of complex chronically ill patients. A person goes to work in a factory, and there are various chemicals in the air. The worker returns home after a full day with a headache and lightheadedness. (This is an alarm response and an indication that the ground regulation system is active and responding to the noxious stimuli.) If the person comes to your clinic on the way home from work, you would likely perform an alarm-state test, but in this instance, there is no problem that warrants an FCT visit, so the cycle goes on for a few days until the worker returns home and is asked by the spouse, "Do you still not feel well after working?"

"I'm doing fine," he replies. "I guess I just needed to get used to it."

The spouse replies, "Oh, that's great! I'm glad it doesn't bother you anymore."

In this case, if the person comes for an appointment, je would likely not show for an alarm disturbance, but for chemical toxicity stresses to various organs, most of them invisible to the patient because it is an adapted response.

This couple goes on a long vacation—two weeks of no work, just play and lots of fresh air. Then it's back to work. Wouldn't you know? The same thing happens again. He gets the headaches, the lightheadedness, and some nausea (an alarm response again), but again, it eventually goes away as the body adapts once more to the work exposures. As the exposures increase, the potential for recovery decreases. Over and over again, a lower standard of balance is achieved. There is increased physical incoherency because more and more energy is required to maintain this adapted state. Maybe when the worker has to put in overtime or extra shifts there are a few symptoms, but eventually these also disappear. The adaptations that have masked the problems for quite some time now give way to maladaptive responses. There are various new symptoms and worsening of complaints. Perhaps it is shortness of breath after exertion, difficulty sleeping, skin rashes, or chronic headaches. It is likely that significant inflammation, hypoxia, and tissue damage is taking place. Now, even a nice vacation doesn't have the same restorative effects.

If you test him at this point, you will see a very different FCT testing pattern that will likely include disturbances to the nerve tissue, neurons, various elements of the central nervous system, several segments of the spinal cord, organs, and tissues...but your patient has yet to come for treatment. The worker also observes that new sensitivities to other stimuli, including food, are not well tolerated. (We mentioned this before briefly and called it the principle of spreading.) While it used to be that every Saturday the worker mowed the lawn with no problem, he now struggles to perform this task because he just doesn't feel well when he fills the lawn mower with gas. Incidentally, we are probably well past the point at which the patient tries supplements and takes medications to help the problem, but if there has been some relief, it is only because the symptoms are being somewhat masked, and these conventional or natural interventions are probably contributing to the downward cycle. The choir might sound a little better in this case because the tenor who couldn't sing on key was kicked out of the group.

There is still another potential phenomenon to keep in mind when the system has been overloaded with toxicity, a phenomenon called switching. While it used to be the case that his main symptoms were headache and brain fog, now it seems that almost anything triggers an itchy rash, loose stools, or shortness of breath. Switching is another very good reason to not think so allopathically about your patient. Of course you want to know what the symptoms are, but I caution you not to be too quick to identify the locus of the problem in the organ that appears to harbor the symptoms. Testing will help to determine the best entry point into the overall state of dyshomeostasis, especially if you're open to being surprised!

Stay with me, dear reader; we're not done yet. Still another variable that is of interest here is that while there are differences between people in terms of their ability to manage toxicological stress, which we might name as the biochemical individuality of response, eventually, everyone can be overwhelmed by toxicity. While differences can be noted, it is also possible that the differences are not explained by the genes, as if it is somehow your fate or destiny. (How's that for a limiting belief system?) These differences may be better explained by so-called epigenetic responses to nutrients and environmental factors or conditions. Let's suppose that this worker was especially blessed with good genes, but his declining health is a sign that he needs more than a good genetic predisposition. The longer the worker waits to come in for an appointment, the more difficult matters become. If the worker has been "coping" through allopathic treatments, including medication, there will be more severe disturbances and potentially more limitations on what your treatment may accomplish. It's not easy.

This worker scenario can be applied to many occupations or toxic home environments. The longer the exposures, the more challenged the patient will be to handle them. If there are additional exposures outside of the workplace, the effects are cumulative. The phenomena of spreading and switching will add to the complexity of the picture when the patient comes to your clinic for help with a long list of symptoms that cross many body systems. Time spent learning about these different stages of health so that you have a conceptual framework in which to place the patient's description of his health problems and your test findings will help you to recognize where he is at and what you're going to try to do about it.

My purpose in giving you these scenarios, variables, and variations is to help you appreciate why each patient is different and to disengage you from any notions that common symptoms would suggest a common treatment. This would be an allopathic approach, and that is not what we intend with FCT testing or treatment. I hope that this description tells you that the situation of a compromised patient is multi-factorial and that the functional status of the patient will be reflected in the responses to FCT filters. Do your best to be clear about what this means. What is it that you are measuring? How will you interpret your ankle-holding activities? Knowing the patient's history and your context for interpreting the FCT testing process can help you. I have found it helpful to make a distinction in my testing between inflammation and tissue damage and interpret this difference to mean a different prospect for response and recovery. The goals of treatment are also probably different.

A Girl with Allergies

Let's consider the most straightforward case first, and then we'll make it more difficult, or ambiguous—you can decide on your own descriptive term after this one. This is the case of a twelve-year-old girl who came to our clinic to be treated for allergies after disappointing responses to various conventional allergy treatments. She was on medication for asthma symptoms. FCT testing showed her to be sensitive to many stimuli, including various chemicals, foods, and outdoor allergens. FCT testing also indicated that she had mostly periodic, but also aperiodic disturbances with significant inflammation to her tonsils, parotid glands, and bronchioles. She did not test for significant tissue damage. According to the testing, she appeared to present a combination of both acute and chronic factors that affected not only these tissues, but the balance of her autonomic nervous system. This was reflected in stress to her olfactory lobe and olfactory nerve, her limbic system, and her hypothalamus.

Long-term chronic exposures to chlorine and solvents from swimming and most likely her home environment combined with a long-term history of antibiotic use as a young child had also manifested in certain aperiodic disturbances within her system and accompanying inflammation. Her system was overloaded by "country living" and daily exposure to allergens, as well as years of antibiotics to treat what was believed to be infection. Any new pollen that blew across their home initiated a new round of symptoms. Moreover, she was almost continually in an alarm phase due to her ongoing exposure to outdoor allergens and her father's use of herbicides to maintain a nice-looking lawn.

The testing identified key toxicants and the organs that were affected, and, through subliminal testing (once again, let's hear it for attention with intention), the sites of greatest inflammation. The testing results clearly showed that the local and regional containment of the stimuli was lost some time ago and that there was significant disturbance and dysregulation of the autonomic nervous system. According to FCT testing, the most important structures to treat were not the sinuses, the ears, the tonsils, or the lung tissues, but her central nervous system, including the olfactory nerve, the olfactory lobe, her emotional center, and the hypothalamus. My hope was that not only would the stress from any toxic influences become invisible to the testing through the FCT treatment, but that there would also no longer be signs of significant inflammation. Here is the key point: If the sources of inflammation could be identified and eliminated, the downward spiral toward tissue damage might also be averted. This would be an indication of a favorable recovery. Loss of hypersensitivity to various stimuli would be possible only if her total body load of burdens was reduced, which was difficult given where she lived. Monitoring her olfactory nerve and other CNS filters was, in my opinion, just as important as the more allopathically chosen tissues like sinuses, ears, tonsils, respiratory tract, and so on. She is doing well.

Woman with Respiratory Complaints

A middle-aged woman came in with respiratory complaints—coughing, shortness of breath, sore throat, and low energy. FCT testing found both periodic and aperiodic disturbances. Her pleura tested for periodic and aperiodic disturbances with inflammation and tissue damage, as did her bronchioles. She was easily triggered into respiratory symptoms by tropical allergens when she went south for the winter. There was also chronic infection from *Streptococcus* and influenza, as well as sensitivity to local molds, especially *Claviceps*. Her central nervous system was further sensitized and stressed by the secondary metabolite, or mycotoxin, produced by a mold called ergot.

In our area of the country, I see ergot commonly as a central nervous system antagonist and find that the body gives high priority to the elimination of its influence as a chemical toxin. Ergot stress can be traced, most importantly, to nerve tissue with other manifestations, including tight muscles (and difficulty holding adjustments), difficulty sleeping, low energy, headaches, and a tendency toward anxiety—a heightened sensitivity to internal and external stimuli—so that the Reticular Formation filter is frequently found to be highly stressed. The patient was only mildly helped by Allegra, but she is doing well because FCT treatment has not only identified triggering incitants, but also those structures that were stressed and sites of inflammation and tissue damage. On her own, she decided to stop using Allegra and other over-the-counter medications because they provided minimal relief and she was encouraged to consider their long-term impact on her overall state of health.

At this point, she continues to come to the clinic twice a year when she's back from Florida. The long-term questions revolve around the concern about the degree of tissue damage. What do I mean? If the cause of the tissue damage has been eliminated, will the body be able to sufficiently repair itself? This means avoiding, or at least reducing the exposure to, environmental toxins and providing the body with adequate nutrition. This also includes helping her body manage the daily exposures to allergens in Florida by taking allergen isodes and nosodes on a monthly basis or as needed to manage total environmental pollutant load. She has also improved her diet and tells me that she doesn't get sick like her friends do.

Regarding the tissue damage, I still saw signs of it in her last FCT test. Many healers, doctors, and researchers have described the existence of various kinds of stress that are present when damage occurs. Sometimes it is described as an interference field, a kind of energetic and often physical scar that may interfere with function. Perhaps in this case, the best that one can hope for is that no further tissue damage takes place because the causes of the inflammation are being treated. At this point, the patient has enjoyed great relief of her symptoms. She is a happy camper. I look forward to testing her again to see if she still tests for residual tissue damage or if the intervention was early enough for sufficient healing to take place that there is little evidence of stress to the most affected tissues.

A Woman with Multiple Complaints

An older woman describes many problems, but her main symptoms are sinus congestion and tingling in the hands and feet. FCT testing indicates that her imbalances include stress to mercury, ergot, *Claviceps*, *Stachybotrys*, dust, and influenza. She also tests for nutritional deficiency. There are periodic disturbances evident in her nervous system, but her pleura tests for inflammation and aperiodic disturbances, including tissue damage. This has come from years of chronic exposure to toxicants, and these are the areas of greatest energy loss and incoherence. In her case, the overall inflammatory pattern is heightened by sensitivities to many foods that she enjoys which are high in amylase. The questions are the same: Can we stop the progression of tissue damage? Can there be a return to a higher state of health? Testing indicates that there are, of course, several degenerative and stressed organs. I find that even if some organs are more obviously damaged and the testing identifies them as degenerative organs, there could be higher value targets accessible through subliminal testing. Sometimes I find them in the central nervous system and the glial cells. Remember the part about near misses, bull's-eyes, and the nagging comment several pages ago?

I continue to refine and experiment with new testing procedures when there are interesting findings, especially when it concerns the tissues and cells of the nervous system. A highly damaged tissue will reflect a diminished functional capacity according to homeostatic criteria and can be split. (Anything can be split.) There is no stronger splitting agent than highly coherent intention. (Did I just say that? More about this subject to follow in a later chapter).

Highly damaged tissues typically match first for tissue damage, followed by inflammation, followed by aperiodic disturbance. Tissues, organs, or nerves that teeter on the brink of tissue damage balance first to inflammation and then sometimes to aperiodic disturbance or a combination of aperiodic and periodic disturbances. In other locations, there will still be filters that are not showing for tissue damage or inflammation, but for dyshomeostasis with periodic disturbances or adapted states. They might be structures of the central nervous system as well as nerve tissue or peripheral nerve filters that test for autonomic dysfunction, dyshomeostasis, and the influence of incitants. I have found that in a case such as this, the body still typically places the highest priority on heavy metal or chemical toxicities. Ask if these problems should be treated first, because I think there are plenty of exceptions for every rule or dogma.

In this instance with the older woman, this meant treating the patient for mercury and ergot, which eliminated her neuropathy and anxiety. Her sleep improved, as did her respiratory symptoms. She carries a dust vial, which she uses on a regular basis to manage sinus and post-nasal drip symptoms that cause a phlegm throat. I see her once a year to check on how she's doing.

I think that these cases give you some tools to better understand your patients, and I am interested in further developments to look at various details of the connective tissue matrix and the amplification of the information in the autonomic nervous system. I think that there are some filter limitations, as I have already frequently mentioned. I simply mean that while the current filters are invaluable, there are others that need to be developed. The most helpful information and results will be obtained from the best-chosen questions, the most accurate filters, and the best targets.

CHAPTER FOUR

Methods of Remedy Creation and Delivery

Dear reader, we are going to do this backward—delivery first, and then creation. I get to. It's my book.

Where Would You Like to Send It?

It's time to move on to another subject. You might be saying to yourself, "What do you mean, 'where would you like to send it?'" By now you've probably developed your own list of places you would like to send me! I mean, where do you want to deliver the remedy to the patient? It occurred to me that if I asked where the best place was to send it, I might actually receive a useful answer. I believe that does happen. Sometimes, rather than delivering the remedy through the mouth, there appear to be better choices. I have given remedies as eye drops, ear drops, and on the skin—when I'm invited to do so and when I ask. Certain tendencies appear that I will share with you for your own exploration.

Here are some examples of instances in which I have sent the information to the eyes: Remedies for allergens, identified through your kits or through the collection of samples (remember that you can make a sample from anything), can be put into the eyes with very good results. I believe the person responds more quickly (maybe more powerfully or completely—I said "maybe") with very good outcomes. Here is a list—not a complete one, but one that includes remedies that I have given through the eyes with, as I said, immediate and powerful results: Pollens, molds, perfume, cosmetic materials, SBS (sick building syndrome), chlorine (and other pool chemicals), Staphylococcus A (for conjunctivitis), and fluorescent light.

Here are some examples of instances in which I have sent information to the ears: Remedies to treat middle– and inner-ear infections for *Streptococcus* work well. (If you remember to ask about where the body would prefer the information to be picked up and the best time for delivery, you can get very specific and presumably more helpful.) I have had good application to this post office box for certain fungal infections, too. Another good example is unwelcomed guests from lakes, rivers, and pools in which the patient's head has been submerged and in communion with all the little critters below the surface, like giardia, cryptosporidium, and ameba. (Even better results can be obtained by applying a principle described earlier in the book to identify the specific critter—the specific ameba or protozoa that is causing the problem—so you deliver a bull's-eye.) These kinds of cases might cause you to reconsider the prospects of swimming in a river or sticking your head under water at a motel or in your own bathtub ever again!

Here are some examples of instances in which I have sent the information to the skin: While the whole story is not necessarily to be found on the surface, fungal remedies can be applied to the affected area with good results. Ringworm is a good example. Cuts that don't want to heal benefit from *Staphylococcus* remedies, but once again, you might want to think about the near-miss discussion to identify what kind of Staph is bothering your patient. You might consider using a sample from the patient (we talked about this earlier—using a patient's fluids—you have choices, so ask) and delivering that message to the surface of the body and maybe via the mouth, as well. You might help some wrestlers or pet owners if you get good at this. If you have a vet in your vicinity that has an appreciation for what you do, you might use her findings to help you to a bull's-eye. You might do it yourself and use a pet sample (saliva, fur, and the other *f* word) to make a remedy that can be applied to the skin. I used to say I would never accept the other *f* sample, but I just couldn't say no. Yes, you're right, dear reader. That really does shed light on yours truly. I told you before, and I meant it: You can make a remedy out of anything. I have also applied remedies directly to the skin of patients with basal cell carcinoma and melanoma with good results.

The point is simple, really: When you are developing your schedule and remedies, you might consider asking which mailbox to send them to and what the best time for delivery would be. As I have said numerous times already, how can you ask about anything that has not crossed your imagination?

How Would You Like to Send It?

This is a topic that is fascinating to yours truly. Dear reader, I don't remember where my idea about this subject came from, but I know it would have been unlikely to have come to the surface without my other training and experiences in Chinese medicine and cold laser therapies. I will try to take you through my thought process so that you will be able to step off my path and to your own when the time is right, and it probably makes a lot more sense after knowing I started processing isodes made from fecal material. Anybody hungry?

A little personal history here might be helpful. Before I got really serious about focusing my practice around FCT testing and treatment, I treated (and evaluated) many patients using the methods of traditional Chinese medicine. Mostly, I treated patients with needles and sometimes included electrical stimulation to enhance the treatments. Many good things happened; however, there were many people, especially children, who were needle-phobic. This led me to explore other methods of engaging the meridian system besides those that I learned about as a student at the American Academy of Acupuncture and Oriental Medicine. I did not think that these obstacles would be overcome by other needling methodologies that I used in my clinic, which included Tong-style acupuncture, Tan meridian balancing, and others, to mention only a few. My good friend and my brother in spirit, Joe Burchik, who is also an acupuncturist, introduced me to other possibilities that used cold laser treatment, which we decided to investigate together. This took both of us on a new journey. It also solidified our friendship and my love for Joe. I learned a lot and am grateful that Joe is now my brother and dear friend. At the time, we spent many hours together talking about the ways we might apply cold laser treatment to help our patients and about how the use of light compared with our needling techniques.

Again, I do not remember anymore what led me to experiment with the cold laser as an alternative delivery system, but I did! I used my FCT testing to develop my understanding of what might be affecting the health of my patients, but rather than delivering the remedy via a drop of a potentized remedy given orally (sending it the usual way), I discovered that the same information could be provided by the light of the cold laser, and the effect was nearly instantaneous. The 635-nanometer light from my Erchonia cold laser was a suitable carrier. I could send the information in the remedy using light as the delivery system. I was excited, amazed, and intrigued…You get the picture. For some time, I continued to experiment with the cold laser delivery of homeopathic information to my patients.

I wanted to understand how this worked, which led me to contact Dr. Bill Tiller. I shared some examples from the clinic with him that resulted in a White Paper that we wrote and appears on his web site. It is called "Importance of a Coherent Delivery System for Homeopathic Remedies," *White Paper XVII.* Feel free to read it. It might encourage you to think about how you would like to send the information to your patient.

I probably could have (or should have) spent the rest of my life exploring this discovery, but apparently that is not in my makeup. I hope this section has made you aware of one more door that you could walk through if it suits you!

CHAPTER FIVE

The World of MEMON

I call it the world of MEMON because it really is a new world to me. I have Dr. Yurkovsky to thank for many things, including introducing me to this technology. At an FCT seminar in White Plains, New York, I met Peter Wydooghe, a wonderful man who represented MEMON and was given the task of making this technology known in places outside of Germany, where it was created by a small group of electrical engineers. I became friends with Peter, and Ardith and I learned about MEMON from him and started to use MEMON products in our clinic. We tested the effects of MEMON transformers and made several interesting discoveries. Our journey with MEMON was also enriched by our friendship and interaction with Mike Bieser. Mike spent time with Peter, also, learning more about its theory and applications. We often talked about what MEMON could do and its potential benefits with Mike. For some time, we worked with Mike to provide MEMON products to our patients, and the value of MEMON technologies is still being explored in our clinic. Like I said, it is its own world.

I can say that ever since I became aware of MEMON, I have considered the importance of eliminating those influences that MEMON can handle. This intent has led to many interesting findings about those sources of incoherency that MEMON can affect.

I have already referred to MEMON a few times in the book to help you think more about how you can bring up discussion of EMFs with your patients. When EMF issues are a problem, you have to try to deal with them, but still be flexible. Don't say to a patient that you won't help him unless he buys all the required MEMON transformers. He might be in new territory with this subject. He might need time to read about it, think about it, budget for it, and convince his wife to go along with it. Often, if you go easy with people about this subject, it gives them the time to purchase MEMON.

I keep MEMON transformers on hand and available in the testing room to use with the patients. Not only does this make it more real for them ("Yes, I do feel better"), it also allows me to monitor the effects of MEMON during the testing. It gives me one more way of establishing its relative importance to the overall picture of health. The use of body transformers, Car B transformers, iPhone transformers, and food harmonizers are included in this aspect of my testing when it is a significant issue. Sometimes I will bring out the dog and pony for this, as it makes not only patients, but you feel good when there can be immediate relief. I like to clear them to these influences at the start of testing because there isn't any part of a person that does not respond in some way to EMFs. Yes, some places of stress are more important than others—higher-value targets. When this has been cleared, it's kind of like sharpening the resolution on your TV. Everything looks better. The testing is cleaner, clearer, and brighter.

You have plenty of available resources to learn all you want about EMF disturbances. That is not the purpose of this book. You also have training from FCT or other sources about the effects of EMFs on human beings. If you are doing FCT, you have also been informed about EMF block, a problem that might interfere with the ability of the remedies to work their magic. When, for whatever reason, I want to help someone that does not have MEMON, I have found it very helpful to make different kinds of EMF-related remedies from FCT filters, environmental isodes collected from home and the workplace, and H vials because taking them immediately before a treatment is helpful, and so is taking them afterward…so is taking them every day. Why guess about the best way when you can test?

EMF environments can also damage remedies. I discovered this with a patient who wasn't clearing, as I like to call it, to a particular problem. After a few tries, we did a little experiment and found that his remedies were affected by his Prius. Shielding the remedies eliminated the problem, and he cleared. He also benefitted from taking a Prius remedy after he got home from work every day since he did not have MEMON. Since this incident, I always wrap the remedies in aluminum foil. Patients are instructed to keep them in foil or store them in a foil-lined container. When it's time for a follow-up appointment, they bring their remedies back. If I don't find the result I'm expecting, sometimes it's because the remedies were not kept in a safe place. With the remedies, it's easy to check. I could start a museum of all of the interesting, unique containers that patients carry the remedies in. I have a veterinarian friend who uses a type of digitally produced homeopathic remedy to treat his animal friends. I told him about the aluminum foil thing, so he decided to try it. He told me the results with his animals are better. It's very fun. Perhaps we should all walk around in aluminum foil to protect ourselves...okay, maybe not.

In an ideal world, when it comes to MEMON you would fix your castle first and then its water supply. Secondly, you would probably start taking care of all the wireless devices that are not plugged into your house—the ones that sit on your lap or next to your pillow or are held near or attached to your noggin. Then you might branch out and fix your car, too. You would harmonize your food and drink. You might even try to harmonize yourself with a body transformer. Dear reader, the world is often far from ideal, so it is good to be practical, too. That is my philosophy, not necessarily that of the MEMON authorities or FCT experts. Like I said, I try to be practical and meet my patient where he is really at.

My experience is that much can be done by harmonizing the phone, harmonizing with the body transformer, harmonizing the food, and prudent usage of the Car B MEMON as your bodyguard. There's so much harmony! I have spent considerable time testing all of the MEMON devices in different circumstances. This has led to many new findings about MEMON, and some of the findings were also surprising to the folks in Germany when Ardith and I shared some of these outcomes with them via Skype. We also developed methods for looking more closely at optimizing the installation of home transformers. We believe that each installation is different, and testing to see that MEMON is doing what it's supposed to do and making the necessary changes is very important. We are pretty good problem solvers in this regard, and we created pictures and different kinds of instructions to help. I think it is far from a plug and play sort of a deal, though.

We have shared some of these findings with other FCT practitioners at seminars and during mentoring sessions. Here are a few things that might help you.

Food Harmonizers are very helpful tools. Many digestive complaints can be eliminated by harmonizing food and drink prior to consumption. I also discovered that if a person forgot to harmonize the meal, in many instances, her symptoms could be quickly relieved by placing the MEMON over the area of complaint. How long ago the meal was eaten will determine the best spot. The patient can easily find it. After all, she is the one with the symptom! Patients who don't have Food Harmonizers are quickly convinced of their value when the timing of the visit is close to a meal that didn't agree with them. When food is an issue, the Food Harmonizer will also reduce stress to many other areas besides the digestive tract, like a particular joint or the ovaries…I'm guessing now. You didn't know about that or consider that? Yes, dear reader, you're welcome.

You probably also didn't consider the idea that the Food Harmonizers could be used to harmonize other materials. I have many wonderful stories about this that involve dental plastics and other dental appliances and materials. I am pleased to say that there are some dentist friends of mine who agree to harmonize dental materials prior to their usage in my patients. When the energetic fit isn't correct, there are plenty of symptoms to pick from: TMJ, headache, sinus troubles, difficulty sleeping, teeth grinding, anxiety—you name it. You can also harmonize medications, supplements, lotions, and cosmetics as long as they aren't stored in metal. If you're not sure if it will work, remember my motto: Why guess when you can test? Again, I'm guessing that unless you were one of the people who heard me speak about this previously, you didn't know about this possibility. Yes, dear reader, you're welcome. Ardith and I don't believe in keeping secrets when it comes to trying to help others. That's what it's about, isn't it?

iPhone Transformers are also very helpful for obvious reasons. Make it real for your patients by comparing the patient's responses with a phone that has a MEMON versus your own. Use any of the techniques that I have already mentioned. There are many good things to read and watch about this topic in relation to cellphones, iPhones, jPhones, kPhones...Where will it end?

Car B Transformers are amazing and incredibly powerful. We don't just give them out like candy because they are very expensive candy. The instructions are inadequate if you intend to use them for anything besides your car. According to our testing, the Car B Transformers can be very helpful (but not perfect) for personal EMF protection when held in the hand or carried in a pocket. All people are different when it comes to sensitivity to EMFs and to the personal use of a Car B Transformer, so you must start slowly, preferably by testing for compatibility. There is the whole continuum: Those who could probably carry one 24/7 and be oblivious to detecting any difference in their own physical, emotional, or mental state, and those who cannot tolerate using it in this way even for a short time. The reasons vary, but some of the places to investigate to make these determinations include signs of stress or damage to the nervous system from heavy metals like mercury, tick-borne illness, and parasites. There are other reasons, too. Even people who are significantly compromised by pathogenic factors such as these can often hold a Car B Transformer for five minutes, three times a day, with great benefit. I encourage you to investigate it for yourself.

The Body Transformers are very fun, too. When your patient is not ready to get or cannot afford a Home Transformer, this device can be of great help, but again, please don't tell them, "It's my way or the highway." According to my testing, the most important influence of the Body Transformer is to significantly increase coherency to the parasympathetic side of the fence. Anxiety is diminished, sleep is often improved, and the heart gets calmer and happier. Stress to the Schumann resonance usually disappears quickly. Go read about Professor Schumann or life in space as an astronaut prior to the installation of generators on ships and stations to improve your appreciation of what this device can do. All of the other previously given advice about making it real applies. Once again, dear reader, you're welcome.

We have a lot of interesting experiences with Home Transformers—both the old ones that you put in the circuit breaker box (although many times our testing allowed us to find a better location) and the new ones that plug into the wall. What could be more simple than that? I'm going to tell you again, though, one last time that it is not just plug and play. It might be simple if all homes were the same, the wiring was correct, and smart meters were actually a good idea. There are many reasons you may need to experiment with the location of the Home Transformer. Ardith spends a great deal of time troubleshooting these installations. Testing samples collected from the homes eliminates the guessing and ensures the problem has been fixed, and sending the patients home with shielded vials that can be exposed in the home allows us to collect information about the EMFs. After the time needed for exposure, the patient reseals it in foil and returns it to the clinic for testing. This does take some time, but when the patient has spent so much money for a product she hardly understands, we think it is our duty to make sure it's working. Yes, one last time, you're welcome. We hope these invaluable secrets will bring good things to you and your patients.

CHAPTER SIX

New Frontiers: The Birth of the H Vial

As I move into the last parts of my book (do I detect jubilation in you, dear reader, like you're getting close to passing a painful stone?), my excitement grows because it is here that my experience of awe and wonder is at its peak. Here we go!

The discoveries around the laser were exciting and very interesting, but my Hawkins-inspired meditations moved me closer and closer to honoring what I would describe as the one light that stands behind and beyond or, better yet, permeates all appearances in the physical plane. Light is possibly only a symbol, too, because the energy that I believe I am working with appears to move faster than the speed of light. It is not effectively shielded by aluminum foil. Yes, that is just one more interesting finding in the clinic! Source energy might be a better term for that which comes from a different domain, as I will try to describe in the pages that follow.

A little background, for starters: For some time, I have calibrated personal experiences and meditations using Hawkins's Map of Consciousness to guide me. Dr. David Hawkins was small in stature, but don't let those shoulders fool you! I also apply these calibrations to my patients, my testing, and the efficacy of my treatments. Having some awareness of the perils and pitfalls, I learned to self-test and self-calibrate, but as has been pointed out to me, this is not without its limitations and potentially erroneous findings!

Most importantly, dear reader, I learned that the more I honored the one Light, the Source energy, in all my patients and in myself, the more the Field (or whatever you would like to call it) demonstrated that it is timeless and independent of locality, just like many others have said or suggested in their own ways. (I'm trying to hit the high points so that anyone who has some acquaintance with these ideas, or is obviously more knowledgeable than me—and that's not too difficult—can easily fill in what I'm leaving out.) The informational fields store anything and everything. We are limited only by our own imaginations and contextual fields about what may be understood differently or recontextualized. We cannot ask about what we cannot imagine. Have I said that enough times by now?

What do I mean by all of this? Well, another new idea and exciting discovery took place in the clinic. Yes, another door was opened. I found that I could imprint my Boston amber round vials with a highly coherent energy field through intention. I could imprint them with a specific meaning concerning a toxin, bacteria, emotion, tissue, or other subject solely by intention. I found that I could imprint these vials with some kind of information that was of very high calibration and gauge the symmetry state. This opened another door that I decided to walk through. I don't think I will ever return. I am very aware of my limited understanding and inadequate theories to explain what I will share with you, and I really do mean this! I've spent a couple of years investigating different ways that I could imprint vials with intention and apply them in the testing and treatment. I attempted to isolate the key components of this process, but simply putting a label with a name on a bottle, similar to the fascinating experiments of Emoto with water, was insufficient to produce these effects. Intention was required to add or transform the words into a useful diagnostic filter or remedy. I believe that my spiritual work enabled me to uncover and express this ability or gift in the clinic, and perhaps every person has the innate ability to do the very same thing.

I do not believe I would have been capable of doing this without working on myself. There is a time and place for everything. I believe the time was ripe for me to move into a realm I never considered when I began doing FCT. After many interesting findings, I decided to contact Dr. Bill Tiller again with the hope that we might be able to find a spot in a larger theoretical framework for this work, as was done with the cold laser discoveries. Perhaps together we will shed some light on these new findings.

To honor the inspiration that I received from Dr. David Hawkins, any vial that I make according to these new methods is an H vial. The designation of H vial reflects my intent that many of my findings and ongoing investigations can be attributed to the time I spent studying David Hawkins's writings. I was present at his final public appearance in Prescott, Arizona not long before he died. I did not know him personally, but I attribute many of my discoveries to his thoughts, which greatly inspire me.

It is very exciting to me that H vials could be potentized and, in my experience, are highly effective—amazingly so—in testing, treatment, and other explorations, too. I'm just getting warmed up! Since I have somehow come to a belief system (by God's grace) that says that I am light, and behind all appearances I only see light or Source energy, a new context for my work in the clinic emerged. I intend to share some of these interesting findings with you, dear reader. I hope these comments will be sufficient to furnish you with enough information to be intrigued, disgusted, or thoroughly disinterested! If you can't relate to the ideas about the H vial, just wait until we get to the discussion of the Source Energy vials! How are you doing with that stone? A book like this one would not make for a good fire, but might be useful for kindling…Just trying to help.

I believe that no devices are required to store intention or send it—none. Zero. Nothing. Perhaps it would be equally plausible to say that there are many possible devices. Human beings can deliver any intention. We do it all the time. I'm just starting to get the hang of it with FCT! My findings are connected to the particulars of my clinic, but that does not suggest that my little tools are required. What are the tools that are required, again? Zip. In FCT testing, the patient holds a metal bar that is connected by a wire to a metal testing platform, and information in the form of homeopathic filters is introduced onto the metal platform to see if it elicits a response. Which part of this is essential? Which tool? I found that I could experience the same responses from patients without the apparatus. Yes, that's right, dear reader. Just grab a hold of their ankles and forget the rest. Go ahead and try it.

I also discovered that the information about the patient's condition was available without the help of the filters. Yes, dear reader, it's the same chorus: Go ahead and try it. I also found that the remedy could be delivered through an H vial, a vial that was never in contact with a homeopathically created remedy. How was it created? Through intent—through an H vial. Thus, the H vial was born. Yes, there's one more chorus: Go ahead and try it. According to my testing, the H vials also affected the physical world, not unlike Bill Tiller's experiments with intention that are described in his books. I wondered what it was about my intent that created the necessary information and delivery system, which was not unlike the laser that I used in my earlier experiments.

For now, MEMON harmonized water in a Boston amber round vial is my intention-storing device. Patients with many different complaints experience nearly immediate relief of various physical and emotional symptoms by using these vials. How do they use them? Which mailbox are they sent to? How should we send them? Excellent results are obtained by taking them through any of the locations already mentioned and also by simply holding them—yes, just holding them. We will save the holding part for later, under the description of Source Energy vials. Are you thoroughly disgusted yet?

The comments of the patients, the subsequent testing sessions, and my own scales (to be discussed soon enough) support my discoveries. I have found it very interesting that applying my intention with varying degrees of attention has helped me to further understand the difference between bull's-eyes and near misses. With God's help and guidance, intention is my mouse and will take me wherever I want to go, always with permission, and create what might be helpful for someone else. These findings also encourage me to explore differences between specific and general intent, detailed and general informational content, and different ways of representing the information. The intent is always to honor the source of any information and to only seek information that honors the Source in someone else. If that is not the case, these doors will close for you. I believe not only that they will close, but that you will take a step backward from the honorable reasons you became involved with FCT in the first place. Yes, I really do mean it. I think what I am alluding to is the most important quality required to do this work. It is about what is in your heart, no matter how smart or experienced you are.

Scales of stress were developed by yours truly, and they were investigated through the H vials, created via intention, for the purpose of identifying and quantifying various stresses or imbalances, including hypertension, acute and chronic pain, susceptibility to allergies, EMF sensitivity, Schumann resonance stress, the largest bio-field distortion, sleep disturbance, anxiety, etc. Dear reader, I'm telling you that I can make a remedy for almost anything…okay, maybe everything. If you ask me if you can do the same, my answer is that I don't know. You will have to do your own work. For me, it has come through the combination of attention and intention, which are inseparable from my spiritual work. I've heard it said that this says something about the difference between a practitioner and a healer. I don't think that distinction is too far off track.

CHAPTER SEVEN

Another New Frontier: Source Energy Vials

This section describes my most recent discoveries...That is, until it is time for another door to appear. My inspiration for this new idea was connected to my work with the H vials and my study of Dr. Bill Tiller's work. I tried to find ways to build a theory to explain my findings and test my theories with further experiments, and I was intrigued by a White Paper written by Dr. Nisha Manek and Dr. Bill Tiller about the sacred Buddha relics. Nisha had come to my clinic a few years earlier for some FCT testing, and I remembered discussing my experiences with FCT and how great men like Bill Tiller and David Hawkins inspired me, so it was very fun and exciting to discover that she'd moved south and was being mentored by Bill while she went to her day job as a rheumatologist. How fun it was to read about her experiments with the relics and the discussion of the effects of the relics on those who visited them and interacted with the monks who took care of them. I encourage you to read the paper. I thought a lot about whether it was the monks or the relics or both that affected the visitors and the space in the room.

The paper encouraged me to keep thinking about how I could share my intentions for health of body, mind, soul, and spirit with others. Could it be embedded somehow in a vial? How specific could it be? Was it better to be not so specific? What about the space in the clinic where I meditated every morning, resulting many times in me believing I was in a meditative state for most of the day? Was this space also conditioned as described by Dr. Tiller in several of his papers? Was this the reason, or part of the reason, that many patients told me how calm it was in that room? Was it more than being in a MEMON-harmonized space? These kinds of questions fascinated me and led me to walk through the last door I am able to describe to you. Some of my favorite conversations about FCT, including this time of discovery, took place with my son Drew, sometimes at the dinner table, sometimes after a game of tennis. I think he found it fascinating. It was memorable for both of us.

Drew and Alyssa were willing participants in my experiments and explorations, as were many of our friends.

I started slowly, trying things in an order that made sense to me. Remember, you can only find what you are open to seeing. In an attempt to better understand what is necessary versus what is simply present, I tried to isolate the necessary components for these effects to take place—it has been an interesting progression—which was a reasonable starting point. Holding vials in my hand while meditating came first. It worked. I found that a vial that was conditioned in this way could be left near an unconditioned vial, and that vial, by the next morning (perhaps earlier), would be conditioned like the first. I found that I could condition a vial that was wrapped in aluminum foil, and that the patient experienced the same effects with a wrapped vial…superluminal speeds, yes! Eventually I found that I did not need to hold the vial, but that I could place my hands on each side of the vial, my hands a few feet apart, while I meditated and could produce the conditioned vial.

Yes, it gets better or stranger by the moment, just in case there is one of you out there who is still bothering to read my book. I found that by placing several boxes of vials on my testing table and meditating with my hands around all of them, all the vials were conditioned. I found that I did not need to use my hands; I could simply focus on conditioning the vials—it was more difficult for me to do, but nevertheless, it was do-able. I found that I did not need the water; I could condition the space or air within the vial and achieve the same effect, which was more easily done if I held the vial in my hand while meditating. I found that if I conditioned a vial that contained the MEMON water (although it probably doesn't need to be MEMON-conditioned water at all), I could take a small amount of water from the vial that I'd conditioned and transfer it to an unconditioned vial or a larger container of water and the unconditioned vial or larger container acquired the same conditioned quality.

I calibrated the room in the clinic according to the Hawkins methods, and it was off the charts. I found that vials made in this way could be taken to other locations or other homes and that the space became conditioned to a more coherent state. Now the door leading to this idea wasn't just opened a crack—it was wide open, and I wasn't going back. Not knowing what to call these vials, I simply referred to these as Hand Imprint vials. I dated them and rechecked them after different periods of time to see how long the changes were measurable. I found the answer to be weeks and months, and probably longer under the right conditions. Dr. Tiller's discussions about the qualities of conditioned space and his work concerning the broadcasting of intent have been very helpful to me. Again, I highly recommend it.

The more I experimented with the vials, the more I realized that the term "Hand Imprint" vials was a misnomer. If something was being altered in my space or within the space of the vial or within me, then it was not about me personally. It was my connection to my Source, to God, and the effects were the manifestation of the energy of the Source. Therefore, I decided to call them Source Energy vials. This feels right to me. Any good things that come from these vials are not about me, but are attributable to the power of intention. I believe that the Source has potentized my intention, expanding or perhaps opening my consciousness so that I can be a conduit of some kind to benefit others. I think this is a consequence of my spiritual work and attests to the powers of attention, attraction, and intention!

I'm trying to make sense of it all and have some ideas about it. According to my testing and marginal intelligence, the realms, or dimensions, beyond the physical realm calibrate at over 1,000 and cannot be calibrated with the Hawkins system. I believe the Hawkins system reflects the material world and ego consciousness, which can be positively or negatively affected by the other domains. Calibration of over 1,000 requires a different system, a different scale, which might be solved by reciprocal numbers using exponentials of the speed of light in the denominator. The use of reciprocal numbers is accepted in my testing as coherent and a meaningful idea or representation. These numbers continue to increase as I move forward, which is another aspect of the relationship between attention, attraction, and intention. The numbers can be matched to elements or dimensions within non-physical domains of emotion, mind, and spirit. I will not get into specific numbers here, just as I did not when referring to the generation of numerical representations of FCT filters in the beginning of the book. Maybe there will be a sequel to this book...Maybe not.

Increasing reciprocal numbers appear to represent increasing frequencies, which might be interpreted as intensification of the Light or Source or Intent. I also think that these increasingly coherent matches represent information from higher realms, though manifestation might be a better description. When I ask about how to locate these increasing numbers, coherency is found in different realms: Initially physical, then emotional, then mental, and now spiritual. There is acceptance of the intuition that each aspect can be considered as a different realm that can permeate other realms (downward causation).

In an attempt to be as global as possible and to operate from as expansive a context as I can fathom (as not to miss what is most important), I continue to try to expand my criteria to engage more completely the overall state of my patients. I am trying to do this without subscribing to anyone else's theories—Western, Chinese, Hindu, etc. I don't want a theory or a clever explanation to constrain me. I don't want to miss what is essential because I have limited my awareness to perceive it. Admittedly, if I perceive something, my ability to comprehend it is again limited by my own limitations! Always! Here, humility is my best friend.

The intention to further understand our unity is a necessary perspective, so that we are not caught up in success in any form. Once the ego gets a hold of anything, it finds a way to make us small and silly, finding our differences, pointing out how special we are, and encouraging any illusions that we are separate. Then, I think it is easy to lose sight of what we are and where we have come from because we have identified so closely with who we are or who we think we are. I will not write any further about some of my ideas trying to describe the nature of the Source Energy vials or how they might work. I am saving that for an intended series of White Papers with Bill Tiller that will hopefully soon be available.

Back to the story: I decided to investigate the possibility of using these Source Energy vials, and I am currently trying to better understand the limitations of sharing Source Energy vials with my patients. This is a work in progress. When I prayed about how to use these vials and asked for guidance and permission to do so, the answer came to me that I should give them by a different method—no drops under the tongue (or anywhere else this time). The patient only needed to hold the vial. Yes, just hold it. For how long? I try to ask to determine this, too, and the answers vary. So do the responses of the patients. With only a couple of exceptions, the responses are overwhelming positive, though. The patient typically expresses her appreciation in less than a minute. She tells me she is calmer and happier, and I am amazed and thankful to God.

Sometimes, after the allotted time, usually five to fifteen minutes, the patient will say, "I don't want to give the vial back. Can I have it?" This led me to start making Source Energy vials for many of my patients. Again, I ask for guidance in all of these aspects, trying to figure out how long they should use it, how frequently, and what time of day the vial can be held. Usually, the answer is before bed. I encourage them to leave the vial in the bedroom to condition the space. According to my testing, it makes a significant difference.

When I am figuring out how long to hold the vial, the answers that come to me vary from five minutes a day to continuously holding it. When people did not follow the advice, there have been a few stressful responses. I don't know why; perhaps you can have too much of a good thing. There may be some connection to a lack of compatibility with the present state of the patient, and it's the wrong time to be holding the vial. I find this fascinating and am in the process of investigating it further. I suspect that there are additional components that may be better appreciated through more insightful questions. Answers can do no more than respond to the limits of any question and context. My current thought is that if the patient is evaluated for the type of incoherencies that are most relevant and can be addressed, a more specific intention (or intention statement) can be delivered to the vial for the person and for the particular incoherency that can be addressed at the present time. Always ask permission so that there is alignment with the Divine Will.

I consistently found that when patients held these vials in their hands, many different things happened: Her headache went away, his stomach pain disappeared, her anxiety evaporated, she felt mentally sharper, his blood pressure dropped, she slept better, he breathed easier, and so on. I used my H vials for different kinds of symptoms, diseases, and stresses to monitor the changes. I also used my FCT filters, which could no longer find matches to particular stressed filters that were identified prior to holding the vial. How am I doing, dear reader, with the readings on your strange and bizarre meter? (I hope the stone will pass soon!) I'm sure that you can appreciate my surprise and excitement.

Another very interesting finding was that an intention vial made specifically for one person would not generate the same findings in another person. I found this reminiscent of Dr. Bill Tiller's discussion about the need to release stored energy from intention devices with the proper intent in his White Paper about the sacred Buddha relics. I found that when a patient holds a vial with a very high-gauge symmetry that was made for another person or with an absence of specific intent, there were not any significant changes despite the high degree of coherence and useful information contained in the vial. I was surprised and intrigued, and I continue to explore the differences between specific and general intent.

The fact that I have made several hundred of these Source Energy vials by now is also an interesting thing to think about. Each one had more attention, stronger attraction, and clearer intention. With each day—yes, each day (this is not an exaggeration; it is measurable)—the vials become more powerful and more coherent and act more quickly. My process of meditation remains the same, so I think it is also about me becoming more and more one with my Source and its manifestation in every aspect of creation. The Source Energy vial is the most powerful remedy that I am using thus far. If the vial is used for a few minutes a day, it will last for at least a few months. Each time it is held, some of its energy is diminished a tiny amount, like a battery. After a few weeks of usage, the patients will tell me they can still feel it, but that it's weaker or takes longer to achieve the same effects. We have patients that like to stop by to recharge the battery!

The patient's state of mind is also a relevant aspect of this experience. What do I mean? I developed H vials for different types of incoherency: Physical, emotional, mental, and spiritual. Each type of incoherency is affected by the Source Energy vial, and their calibration with the Map of Consciousness is also temporarily raised. Patient comments after holding the Source Energy vial and the H vial measurements indicate that in addition to physical complaints, negative feelings, negative thoughts, and even negative belief systems can be engaged. A very interesting aspect of these findings involves the ability of a person who is engaged in negative thinking or intending to negate good intent. I am reminded of a quotation that I believe is often attributed to the melancholy Dane, Soren Kierkegaard, who said, "Man's ability lies in his freedom to say no." There have been some interesting examples of this freedom, perhaps better described as small mindedness, to utter a no.

When I talk with my patients who have held these vials, they ask me what is in the vial. How would you answer that? I say something like this: We are body, mind, and spirit, but what describes us best is that we are spirit. What you have been holding honors the source of your existence. (As David Hawkins often said, we are spiritual beings subject only to what we hold in mind.) I need to hold in mind only what I believe honors what you are and where you have come from. I intend to be of help to you, sometimes intending very specific things and sometimes intending more general things. It depends on what is happening between us today in the context of our conversation and testing. When I hold the vial to make a Source Energy vial, this is my intention, but I also think, "Thy will be done." You might be wondering if you could make these vials. I don't know why not. Go back and reread what I said about the H vials for my best advice to you about opening this door.

On rare occasions, moving forward by intuition and guided by love and compassion for the patient, I might express some other thoughts that might be of benefit. Maybe I can help him think differently about the experience of his illness, because being ill can bring new perspective. For example, maybe it is time to surrender a painful piece of history and all of the baggage that goes with it. This is discoverable in testing, but it is up to the patient to decide if it is time to explore it. It is always about timing—I think that it is the right time when it is the right time. Why is it the right time now? Because it is the right time. I really enjoy thinking in this way. Thanks, David Hawkins. It is this way because it is this way according to a timing and rhythm that I do not understand and thankfully am not in charge of! I try to meet each person on his terms, honoring the light in each person and not identifying with the content, but intending from a higher context and level of consciousness. That is one way of describing the state that I seek to hold on to, to intend—not only at the clinic, but wherever I am. I try to intend from a place of unity, a place that it is love, peace, and joy, a state that ensures that despite all perceptions and exaggerations of differences, we are one.

When any ideas of how special or different we are intrude into our thinking, it is a field day for foolish thinking and story weaving to suit small-minded purposes, and we are missing the opportunity to be present and open to learning the next lesson in the classroom of this life. I believe this is projected in my thinking, testing, and treatment of patients. Think about how foolish it is to stay small by exaggerating our differences; as if we know the difference between what things actually are and what they appear to be.

Think about what I'm saying the next time anyone gets under your skin. It tells us a lot about ourselves and not too much about them. You could just be content with the idea that you are in a different place, thinking and operating and intending from a different world and a different context. You might be in the same room, but you are not in the same place, not on the same map.

The courage to let go of our special exemptions to remain small and special opens the doors to no longer being wedded to an outcome. How does the saying go? "Father, forgive them, for they know not what they do." Father, forgive them, for they are clueless. In my moments of cluelessness (you may wonder if I am going for the record), I find peace in the context of my life, for it shapes and defines the content. I am light, and all I see is light, for behind every appearance, including my own, there is only light. The courage to surrender that which holds us back and our investment in an outcome allows us to be in the moment and truly present, willing to learn and expand our consciousness according to the will and divine intention of our Source. What did Jesus say about faith even the size of a mustard seed?

I think I am learning to surrender ambition and professional agendas, but perhaps, dear reader, you will find me to still be quite clueless. That is okay. I wish you well in your FCT journeys and the self-discovery that goes with it. As for me, I believe that everything is permeated by the Source energy that originates from a much higher and timeless space and placeless place. Yes, all is made in the image of God. Everything is occurring or unfolding perfectly in its accorded time or karma, and that becomes good enough for me. Yes, it is what it is because that is what it is. Perfect. I intend to use what God has given me to honor the light that I now see in all the manifestations from the Source. It's all very practical! Judgments and comparisons have given way to compassion and joy in the unfolding of all appearances.

Now there is only the light, and beyond every appearance, including all the appearances in my clinic, there is only the light. Thanks be to God. It is in these moments that I am fully engaged by intention with love, peace, and joy in my heart that the Source Energy vials are created.

These closing comments, which are part meditation, part homily, and part invitation, are intended to honor the one Light that stands behind and beyond the reader and writer.

I hope that by sharing my FCT adventure with you, good things will happen. That is the intention of every page of this book. Where is the work leading me? Oh, that's right. I already said it. It leads me to exactly where I need to and get to go. Like I said, it's a one-way ticket until I hear the chariots. It is this way because it is this way. Peace.

CONCLUSION

Meditation

My book is finished with the sharing of the meditation that has guided me in its creation. The meditation has informed my attention, fueled my attraction, and guided my intention.

This is the day the Lord has made. Let us rejoice and be glad in it. Let us give thanks for the gift of the Light, for it is the Light that makes us One. All has come from the Light, and one day all will return. Let us give thanks for the gifts of faith, hope, and love, for when the Light has come into our lives, the world is forgiven and there are no grievances about anyone or anything, for any reason, known or unknown. Future, present, past, or karmic, it matters not, for in the brilliance of the Light, our spiritual vision is restored. We honor the one Light that stands behind and permeates every appearance, including our own. We give thanks for the gift of peace that comes to us when we surrender every negative emotion, every negative thought, every negative intent, and every limiting belief system that would keep us small. We intend love, joy, and peace toward all, so by the power of intent and the grace of God, let us walk in the Light, reflect the Light, and become one with the Light, for the Light is our source, our destination, and our home. For I am not a body, I am an infinite being subject only to what I hold in mind and still as God intended me to be and to become. Thy will be done. Amen.

A very brief introduction by Simon Rees, ND

Establishment and Teaching of FCT

Field Control Therapy, or FCT, was founded in 1999 as a system of intelligent integrative medicine by Savely Yurkovsky, MD, a Ukrainian-born board-certified cardiologist who since 1984 has maintained a clinical practice and a writing schedule in New York. After investigating many branches of conventional and alternative medicine, Dr. Yurkovsky ingeniously sought to apply universal systems principles of science to the process of deciding which modalities to integrate and how. He was driven to do so by the ill health of his own son and many patients and his horror at the dismally inconsistent results and frequent failure of modern medicine. FCT has been studied and put into clinical practice by students around the world, including medical doctors, chiropractors, dentists, nurses, homeopaths, acupuncturists, and naturopathic doctors.

Overview of FCT

FCT has four main aspects:

1. Living Systems: A new theoretical model of health based on systems science.

2. Bioresonance Testing: A new diagnostic approach emphasizing "information fields."

3. Information Medicine: A new therapeutic approach emphasizing "information fields."

4. Disease Causation: A problem-solving clinical algorithm.

FCT in Layman's Terms

FCT is a form of what is popularly nicknamed "energy medicine;" at least, that is a term that some would apply to it, although in technical terms, it would be more accurate to say "information medicine." It deals with the energetic aspects of human physiology in health and disease and corresponding energy-based methods of diagnosis (using a technique called "bio-resonance testing") and treatment (using energy-imprinted water). In physics, the domain of "information" or "information fields" is, technically speaking, different from energy and represents a more accurate scientific description of what FCT focuses on. Another term some have therefore applied in a loose layman's sense is "subtle energy fields." The clinical application of FCT is guided by a priority-based case analysis and series of steps using principles drawn from systems science and disease causation. This leads to an understanding of health and disease based on a focus on the twin notions of "key toxins" and "key organs." For example, by focusing on toxins such as mercury on the one hand and organs and tissues such as the bone marrow on the other, outstanding clinical results are achieved in even the most apparently "incurable" and "unexplained" severe pathologies. System properties are paramount. The body is recognized as an intelligent, self-managing system—hence, it is not necessary to treat it as a passive recipient of medical substances; instead, an emphasis can be placed on delivering "intelligence" in the form of information fields (i.e., inputs from a domain of high influence). Further, the emphasis extends to focusing on inputs of fundamental priority (i.e., inputs of high meaning).

Brief Example

As an example, let us imagine that a patient with Multiple Sclerosis (M.S.) has dental mercury toxicity in the bone marrow and in the myelin sheath of the nerves and tapeworm in the bowel. These will very likely have gone previously undetected and unsuspected. It may also be—as in real cases of this type—that the M.S. was worsening prior to FCT and then turned a corner under FCT care, leading to a full recovery. FCT may detect the information fields of mercury in a state of energetic resonance with a patient's bone marrow and myelin sheath and of tapeworm in relation to the bowel, respectively, and so may correspondingly lead to the delivery of information fields derived from signals of mercury, bone marrow, myelin sheath, tapeworm, and bowel held in a water medium.

These will not be delivered in isolation, as typically there will also be other key organs—including organs of elimination such as the kidneys—needing to be included in a sequential organ treatment plan. Many other organs and pernicious factors might alternatively have come up during the bio-resonance testing, but the focus of the test steps is aimed at priority layers. Priory is evaluated in systems terms. For example, the bone marrow might not seem very connected with M.S. at first glance—until you remember the blood production that takes place there and realize that everything in the body is interconnected. In a systems perspective, treating the bone marrow holds high meaning to the global system.

What Takes Place in an FCT Consultation

FCT is carried out in the office via a consultation of typically an hour or ninety minutes. First, the patient is interviewed regarding their current symptoms and case history, with special attention to certain things such as environmental toxicity exposures and general systemic health markers. Second, the case is analyzed by the practitioner in relation to systems science. Third, the patient lies down on their back for twenty to thirty minutes, fully clothed except for shoes, and a non-invasive muscle-testing procedure is carried out at the feet. This is a process known as bio-resonance testing, used to establish the current priorities and remedies for the treatment plan. Afterward, the corresponding remedy bottles, instructions, and advice are shared with the patient to take home, and a follow-up test arranged to take place typically after a few weeks.

What Is the Aim of Delivering "Information Fields" to Organs, and What Do They Do?

These information fields have no direct medical action in the body (in the normal understanding of medical action as directly affecting or altering pathways or functions). However, they are aimed at providing physiologically nourishing "intelligence"—that is, information-field constituents—that may assist the organs and tissues (such as, in our example case, the bone marrow and myelin sheath) in their own self-management. By way of parallel, food does not have a direct medical action, but instead provides the organs and tissues with nourishment that assists in their self-management, with the difference that whereas food provides required biochemical constituents, FCT provides required information-field constituents.

FCT could therefore be broadly considered a form of "informational" nutrition based on the notion that in addition to food, water, and air, our organs also require information-field inputs to help sustain them. (In fact, pursuing this analogy may lead us to consider—as my teaching and writing colleague Kevin Eakins, ND has astutely put it—that all forms of disease are in essence "information deficits.") As an open system, the human being derives these information-field inputs all of the time from its environment (another way to put this is what we are constantly learning—or becoming more intelligent physiologically—from our environment). FCT "tops this up" with enriched and targeted informational inputs. As a side benefit, the organs then tend toward better health, which frequently leads to reduction in symptoms and resolution of health problems, but—just like food, water, and air—FCT inputs do not themselves achieve these things; the body does that through improved self-management.

Definition of FCT in Technical Terms

1. **The Paradigm of Living Systems**: Perspective, Priority, Essence, the Nature of Reality.

Systems: A patient is a living system. A living system is an intelligent, self-managing, complex, organized whole consisting of many parts (sub-systems) that dynamically interact.

Paradigm Analysis: These observations represent a fundamental shift in paradigm in medicine. The "Systems View of the World" (named as such by author Ervin Laszlo) represents a groundbreaking thread of ideas that Kevin Eakins and I have named the "Living Systems Revolution" (as discussed on our blog at www.livingsystemsrevolution.com), which is in the process of radically transforming medicine, science, and society. Some of the many aspects of this revolution of ideas involve the network-like interconnectedness of everything at the level of information fields and the self-managing intelligence inherent in systems everywhere.

The Over-Specialization Syndrome: This has been identified as one of the principle causes of a lack of scientific progress and resolution of many collective dilemmas, including the health crisis afflicting society.

The Eight Guiding Principles: To gain superior clinical results, the systems emphasis targets essential "leverage" points of the system (such as bone marrow), fundamental domains of physiology (i.e., information fields), and underlying disease causes (such as mercury). These and other clinical imperative can be summarized as perspective; priority; essence; meaning; individuality; safety; health; and collaboration.

Science: FCT seeks to be genuinely scientific rather than contradicting established scientific knowledge as orthodox medicine and other forms of medicine do by ignoring knowledge, e.g., from physics and toxicology.

The Twelve Key System Properties: Before applying a key to a lock, Dr. Yurkovsky has insisted on the need to study the lock first. FCT is based on the properties of living systems: Intelligence, identity, purpose, dynamism, unity, interconnectivity, openness, equilibrium, complexity, nonlinearity, individuality, diversity.

Systems Criteria of Science and Success: To evaluate how scientific an approach is, and how successful, systems science demands a new set of criteria that are not normally applied in medicine outside of FCT. This includes the need to evaluate the overall state of the whole system and the need to do so over a long period of time.

2. **The Power of Informational Fields**: Physics, Bio-resonance Testing, and Information Medicine

Information Fields and Intelligence: In physics terms, there are three constituents to everything: Matter, energy, and information fields. An analogy, in the building of a house, is the bricks and mortar (matter), construction workers (energy), and house plan (information fields). The same domains are applicable in the living body. Of these, information fields are by far the most powerful domain in its influence on health, as physiological intelligence largely governs the other two. It therefore forms the primary clinical focus of FCT.

Matter-Energy-Information Inputs: All forms of medicine are in essence inputs into these three domains.

Information Medicine: In FCT, information fields relating to organs and pernicious factors are encapsulated in a water carrier medium in sealed glass vials to be used in the diagnostic and therapeutics.

Bio-resonance Testing and Isopathy: By "diagnostics" and "therapeutics" we do not refer to the identification or treatment of disease labels, but to the investigation of the information-field status of organs and nutritional provision of information fields to them. On a diagnostic level, the main method is the one known as "bio-resonance testing," in which information field signals, held in hundreds of glass vials, are used to investigate the information-field responses of different organs. On a therapeutic level, the main method is one we call "information medicine." Philosophically it has links with its cousin "homeopathy" and especially a branch known as "causative homeopathy" or "isopathy." Inputs are given to key internal organs at the level of information fields. It is not an active treatment of any disease condition or symptom or organ, but comprises the use of information fields to nourish and assist organs informationally and thereby improve their self-management.

3. The Precision of Disease Causation: Digital Forensics, Key Toxins, EMFs, Infections, and Lifestyle

Disease Causation: In its efforts to assist the body in its self-management in a civilization with widespread bio-accumulative toxicity, FCT places an emphasis on seeking to identify and help the organs to safely remove the key pernicious factors (especially toxins) that undermine health and to identify, assist, and protect the specific organs and tissues affected—with particular attention to those organs playing key systemic roles—and to do so intelligently, safely, and effectively.

FCT as a Problem-Solving System and Detective Process: "Digital forensics" is used to achieve the goals of "causative medicine." This involves identifying patterns in the field responses of specific organs and tissues such as bone marrow, kidneys, adrenal glands, etc. and pernicious factors such as mercury, lead, candida, giardia, electromagnetic fields, etc. as well as an in-depth investigation of environment and lifestyle.

Eight Central Theories of Health and Disease in FCT: The view of health and disease taken in FCT is based on systems science, and the following eight theories touch on a number of key aspects:

Theory of Health and Disease as an Interface, Theory of Bioaccumulative Toxicity-Based Disease, Theory of Key Toxins, Theory of Key Organs, Theory of Five Key Organ Systems, Theory of Organ Protection, Theory of Non-Disease Treatment of Disease, and Theory of Multi-Factorial Disease.

Testing Algorithm: Based on the above theories, the diagnostic arm of FCT follows a precise algorithm of testing. This comprises a patient interview and systems-based case analysis followed by a half-hour series of non-invasive body interrogations using bio-resonance testing. The process is modeled on the twin notion of disease as relating to the interface between organs and pernicious factors and on the quest to establish key organs and key toxins. The objective of the algorithm, each time a test is conducted in the clinic, is to establish which out of the hundreds of possibilities are the information-fields of key organs and pernicious factors involved in a given moment and which corresponding remedies and advice are therefore indicated. Testing flows directly into the creation of a sequential treatment plan, which is normally read to write out and provide to the clinic to take home after the test. The client will then typically spend a few days completing the treatment plan, then return to the clinic after a few weeks for a re-evaluation because the testing algorithm proceeds in a layered, prioritized fashion, and it is not possible to address everything in one go.

Glossary of Terms

The purpose of the glossary is to provide you with simple definitions—a little help, if you will—to make your way more easily through my book. These are not intended to be exhaustive definitions. Referring to the glossary will help you to understand what *I* mean when I am using these terms, because they have been variously defined and expounded upon by others. There are plenty of resources that you may read if you want to investigate any of these terms in greater depth or detail. At the end of the book you will find a list of Suggested Resources that may help you to increase your understanding and appreciation of these terms.

The glossary is divided into two parts: Terms that are specifically relevant to Field Control Therapy and other significant terms that are used in my book. *For those of you who are new to Field Control Therapy*, an appendix has been included to introduce you to its basic theory and practice. You might find it helpful to read the appendix before jumping into Chapter 1.

Terms Relevant To Field Control Therapy (FCT)

Algorithm. A method, set of rules, or instruction used in FCT to test the patient.

Cleared or clearing. A stress identified by the testing process has been eliminated.

FCT Moves. The tester's actions of placing different filters on the platform in response to the patient's response to various filters during testing. These "moves" are intended to collect additional information by adding new filters to the platform to find additional relevant organs, tissues, toxins, infections, etc. that are affecting the patient. For more information, you can look into the FCT-related resources at the end of this book.

FCT Testing Apparatus. The testing apparatus consists of three parts: A metal rod held in the dominant hand of the patient, a metal platform upon which the filters (testing vials) are placed, and a wire that connects the rod to the platform.

Filters. Testing vials that contain water that has been potentized with a substance by a homeopathic process. These filters are placed on the platform during testing to determine the significance of a particular substance (organ, tissue, infectious agent, toxin, etc.). The testing process eventually creates a protocol of homeopathic remedies to be given in a particular order and time frame.

Filters: Degenerative Organ Filters. There are five degenerative organ filters in FCT. These are considered to be the most important organs or tissues to be considered for FCT treatment because they are the most damaged organs. These five filters are identified numerically, in their order of importance, beginning with the most important degenerative organ, simply named degenerative organ number one. These filters are made to varying potencies of parasympathetic nerve tissue.

Filters: Stressed Organ Filters. There are ten stressed organ filters in FCT. These are considered to be very important indicators of significant stress to the patient. However, these ten filters are of secondary importance to the degenerative organ filters. Like the five degenerative organ filters, the ten stressed organ filters are identified numerically in their order of importance, beginning with the most important stressed organ, simply named stressed organ number one. These filters are made to varying potencies of sympathetic tissue. These fifteen filters (degenerative and stressed) form the backbone of the FCT algorithm (method) for evaluation of what aspects of the patient should be the primary focus of the testing and treatment. There are other organs that can be included for good reasons, but that is beyond the scope of this simple definition. I kindly refer to these fifteen filters as the Lords because of their central role in the theory and practice of FCT testing and treatment, and no offense is intended.

Filters: Master Filters. These filters are created to include relevant information for more than one filter. For example, a master filter might include the filters for several heavy metals or several viruses, not just a single metal or virus. These master filters can help you to find your target area before zeroing in on the bull's-eye. For example, the master vial would tell you if the problem you were investigating was caused by a virus or a metal but not the particular virus or metal. In this case if you determined from the master vial that it was a metal problem then you would take the next step of identifying what particular metal was the cause of the problem. Determining that the problem was a metal ensured that you found the target. Identifying the particular metal means you have found the bull's eye. (I often like to refer to master filters as global or umbrella filters because of the usefulness of first assessing the patient's concerns from a more inclusive perspective.)

Filters: Test Filters. Test vials that contain information created through homeopathic methods to test the patient. Bio-resonance testing is used to determine whether or not the test vial has significance for the patient by the presence of or lack of a match (or resonance).

Isode. A homeopathic remedy that is made from a pernicious agent (toxin, virus, heavy metal, cellphone emission, allergen, etc.) or an environment that may contain harmful pathogenic factors (urine, stool, saliva, well water, exhaust emission, the air in a barn, etc.).

Mapping. Using the various test filters within FCT to conduct an overall evaluation of different aspects of the patient's health that may require additional testing and potential treatment. This is typically done during an initial visit. For example, the patient may show evidence through bio-resonance matches that there is stress to antibiotics, vaccines, viruses, heavy metals, parasites, EMFs, etc., and all of these stresses cannot be treated at the same time. The test findings might indicate that the largest stresses are to bone marrow, kidneys, hypothalamus, liver, and striated muscles but that there are many other organs that are stressed, as well. The particular stresses and the causes of these stresses will be identified through the testing process (algorithm), as well as, just as importantly, what should be treated first. Mapping gives the tester many clues about what may arise during subsequent tests and require treatment.

Match or matching. This is what bio-resonance testing is all about! A stress created by the placement of a test filter on the platform is felt by the practitioner using the FCT muscle testing process. The tester finds a second filter that matches the initial stress response. For example, the stress that is produced by placement of the first degenerative organ filter is negated by the addition of a second filter—for example, bone marrow. A match between the first degenerative organ filter and bone marrow has been found, so the tester concludes that the first degenerative organ is bone marrow and will make a bone marrow remedy of the proper potency to match the degree of stress that is reflected in the test.

Platform. This is a small rectangular block of metal upon which the filters are placed. The platform is connected to a wire that is connected to a metal rod that is held by the patient.

Remedy. This is a vial with water that has been potentized homeopathically to a particular strength (potency).

Sarcode. This is a homeopathic remedy that is made from an organ or tissue.

Split or Splitting. When a match has been created through one of the FCT moves, the patient no longer tests to be in a "stressful" state according to the FCT muscle testing procedure. Additional vials are added to the platform, producing a new stress. According to FCT theory, this new stress reveals additional relevant factors that are required to understand the overall stress and health of an organ or tissue.

Other Important Terms

Abelian algebra. There is an abundance of information about Abelian algebra, from algebra textbooks to the Internet. In this book it is mentioned for the purpose of informing the reader that the order of introducing filters onto the platform makes a significant difference in the test results and conclusions about the findings. While a+b = b+a, or a x b = b x a, in FCT testing there are differences in responses to the filters depending on the order of placement on the platform. (Volume Two will likely add to this definition.)

AK = Applied Kinesiology. Knock yourselves out and read the many different textbooks on the subject! Here, I will simply state that there are many AK methods to investigate the patient's responses to various AK approaches that share common mechanisms through various techniques that are not fully understood. These methods bypass the conscious mind and engage the unconscious realm to elicit information not readily available through conventional methods. In FCT, this involves a kind of muscle testing that does not rely upon a physical challenge of a strong (intact) muscle, but a non-force response that is experienced through the holding of the patient's ankles.

Alarm State. This is a period of time in which the patient is in a stressful state in response to a stress of some kind.

Aperiodic Disturbance. This is a condition that exists when a patient has been exposed to a stress that does not immediately produce an obvious experience of stress for the patient.

Coherency. Time to go read about the many aspects of this word if you'd like! In this book it mostly refers to a state in which conflicts, irregularities, or disturbances are diminishing or being eliminated and in which there is an increasing level of unity or oneness in many different domains.

Downward Causation. This is a theory that the creation of all things begins from above, in a non-material realm, with the final manifestation being the physical universe—and yes, there are many interesting ideas around this general notion.

EMF=Electromagnetic Field. In this book, the use of the term is relevant for a few reasons; the most important reason for its presence in the book is the influence of technology on health. FCT identifies several sources of EMFs that affect health, including cellphones, computers, and fluorescent lights. Here again, for the interested reader, there are many wonderful resources.

H Vial. This is my designation for a filter that has been created for a specific organ, tissue, pathogenic factor, or concept without the use of a substance (made by intention).

Iatrogenic Factors. This term refers to any medication, treatment, or test that has left some stressful artifacts to the patient. These factors can be identified through testing and cleared through the administration of a remedy.

Intact Muscle. In AK, this refers to a muscle that remains strong against a physical challenge. For more information, consult any applied kinesiology text.

Kidney 27. This is an acupuncture point located on the chest. Its specific location is on the lower border of the clavicle, 2 *cun* lateral to the anterior midline.

Map of Consciousness. This is David Hawkins's depiction of the levels of consciousness. Please read his many insightful books about his theories—some of my favorites are listed at the back of the book as recommended reading.

Mental Radiesthesia. In this book, the main point to be made is that there are qualities of interaction with oneself and the environment that appear to have their origin within the subject, or the person who is involved in some activity that engages these aspects: Energy, information, spirit, etc.

Physical Radiesthesia. In this book, the main point to be made is that there are qualities that come from, or appear to come from, the physical universe, and these qualities may extend beyond conventional methods for measuring their presence and significance.

Ren Meridian. This is an energetic line described by Chinese medicine that runs down the midline of the anterior side of the body. To learn about its precise trajectory and significance, please consult a textbook in acupuncture.

Schumann Resonance. This is an important term in this book because it appears to be connected to a primary cycle in the body. When the astronauts first went into space and orbited Earth outside the ionosphere, there were significant effects to their health. Many years prior to space travel, a German professor named Schumann (you knew that was coming!) studied the effects of living below the surface of Earth with his students. In between the surface of Earth and the ionosphere, a standing wave is created. It has several peaks, but the primary peak fluctuates at around 7.39 hertz. This frequency is important to our health and is affected by geopathic stress. A disturbance of this kind especially affects the parasympathetic mechanisms that are especially important during non-waking hours.

Source Energy Vial. A vial that I have created through intent. The intent of this vial is echoed in the meditation toward the end of my book. The intent that is imprinted may be general or very specific, with a particular intention for a particular patient. The use of the term Source Energy is intended to designate that the qualities that are placed into the vial are not personal, but a reflection of certain universal qualities that all human beings share.

Two Pointing. If you would like a detailed discussion of this idea, please refer to an applied kinesiology textbook. In this book, it refers to the use of matching in a manner that combines the findings of FCT testing with the application of AK methods to localize a stress (organ, tissue, or pathogen) and match it with a location on the body of the patient.

Upward Causation. This refers to the theory that the creation of all things begins with a physical substance, particle, sub-atomic particle, or sub-sub-atomic particle—you get it—and everything else comes as a consequence thereof, as some kind of epiphenomena. Just think from the bottom up!

VOC=Volatile Organic Chemicals. Yes, there are lots of them, and more found every day.

Yin Tang Point. This is an acupuncture point located midway between the medial ends of the eyebrows.

Suggested Reading

Diamond, John. *Facets of a Diamond: Reflections of a Healer.* Ridgefield: Enhancement Books, 2003.

Emoto, Masuru. *The Healing Power of Water.* Carlsbad: Hay House, Inc., 2004.

Fraser, Peter H., Harry Massey and Joan Paris Wilcox. *Decoding The Human Body-Field. The New Science of Information as Medicine.* Rochester: Healing Arts Press, 2008.

Fraser, Peter H. *Energy and Information in Nature. A Collection of Papers on the NES Health Theory of the Human Body Field.* Poole, UK: Choice Point Communications, 2012.

Hawkins, David R. *Power Vs Force. The Hidden Determinants of Human Behavior.* Sedona: Veritas Publishing House, 1995.

Hawkins, David R. *Truth Vs Falsehood. How To Tell The Difference.* Carlsbad: Hay House, Inc. 2005.

Hawkins, David R. *Reality and Subjectivity.* Sedona: Veritas Publishing House, 2003.

Hawkins, David R. *Reality, Spirituality, and Modern Man.* Toronto: Axial Publishing Company, 2008.

Hawkins, David R. *The Eye Of The I. From Which Nothing Is Hidden.* Sedona: Veritas Publishing House, 2007.

Hawkins, David R. *Transcending The Levels Of Consciousness. The Stairway To Enlightenment.* Sedona: Veritas Publishing House, 2006.

Hawkins, David R. *Healing and Recovery.* Sedona: Veritas Publishing House, 2009.

Hawkins, David R. *Letting Go. The Pathway of Surrender.* Sedona: Veritas Publishing House, 2012.

Ho, Mae-Won. *The Rainbow And The Worm. The Physics of Organisms.* Hackensack: World Scientific Publishing Company, 2008.

Ho, Mae-Won. *Living Rainbow H20.* Hackensack: World Scientific Publishing Company, 2012.

Mundy, Jon. *Living a Course in Miracles. An Essential Guide To the Classic Text.* New York: Sterling Ethos, 2011.

Pischinger, Alfred. *The Extracellular Matrix and Ground Regulation. Basis for a Holistic Biological Medicine.* Berkeley: North Atlantic Books, 2007.

Rea, William J. and Kalpana D. Patel. *Reversibility of Chronic Disease and Hypersensitivity. Regulating Mechanisms of Chemical Sensitivity. Volume 1.* Boca Raton: CRC Press, 2010.

Rea, William J. and Kalpana D. Patel. *Reversibility of Chronic Disease and Hypersensitivity. The Effects of Environmental Pollutants on the Organ System. Volume 2.* Boca Raton: CRC Press, 2014.

Tiller, William A. *Science and Human Transformation: Subtle Energies, Intentionality, and Consciousness.* Walnut Creek, CA: Pavior Publishing, 1997.

Tiller, William A. *Psychoenergetic Science: A Second Copernican-Scale Revolution.* Walnut Creek, CA: Pavior Publishing, 2007.

Tiller, William A., Walter E. Dibble, and Michael J. Kohane. *Conscious Acts Of Creation: The Emergence Of A New Physics.* Walnut Creek, CA: Pavior Publishing, 2001.

Truman, Karol. *Feelings Buried Alive Never Die.* St. George: Olympus Distributing, 1991.

Walther, David S. *Applied Kinesiology.* Shawnee Mission: Triad of Health Publishing, 1988.

Helpful websites:

Rees, Simon and Kevin Eakins. www.livingsystemsrevolution.com. This website contains information about FCT and related subjects.

Tiller, William A. www.tillerfoundation.org. This website contains Dr. Tiller's white papers and other information about his work.

Yurkovsky, Savely A. www.yurkovsky.com. This website contains extensive information about FCT written by its founder.

Disclaimer

Writing an objective disclaimer should probably be assigned to someone besides this author for reasons that will likely become obvious during the reading of my book. Nonetheless, it is probably at least prudent to say that information medicine (for lack of a better term) is not comparable to energetic medicine and certainly not to conventional medicine. Even the use of the term "information medicine" is problematic, but perhaps it is a catalyst to encourage the movement toward a different way of describing either health or its absence. Maybe even the use of the word "medicine" needs to disappear when it comes to the subject of information medicine or Field Control Therapy! However, in the here and now of our present culture, and to be as clear as possible, it needs to be said that the contents of this book have more to do with "informational matters" that have little to do with the focus or practice of conventional medicine. Therefore, it is easy to say that this book is not intended to give medical advice in any conventional sense of the word or to serve as a replacement for its recommendations.

In our clinic, we make this clear and ask our patients to initial statements to the same effect. Let me try to say it even more plainly: *This book is not a medical textbook, nor does it intend in any way to give medical advice*. The contents of this book are not intended to replace or diminish any findings or treatments that are currently rendered by conventional medicine. I hope that this disclaimer covers this topic for all of you who are interested in my book: Practitioners, patients, like-minded souls, and quack watchers.

Finally, I want to say one last time that the contents of this book have been developed through my own work and personal exploration of FCT. The methods, and the concepts used to develop the methods, as well as the interpretation of the findings, are my own. The book is not intended to be an exposition of current FCT theory and practice.

www.ingramcontent.com/pod-product-compliance
Lightning Source LLC
LaVergne TN
LVHW051839080426
835512LV00018B/2971
* 9 7 8 1 9 4 6 1 9 5 9 1 3 *